Praise for *Clear*

"Jean Haner is a brilliant
laboratory of her own body
Clear Heart—and you will
are challenged by the ene
recognized. This book is a
aware of these energies bu
And I am so relieved that .

le

e

workers and healers who often 'pick up' energy from their clients."

—**Donna Eden**, author of *Energy Medicine: Balancing Your Body's Energies for Optimal Health, Joy, and Vitality* and co-author of *The Energies of Love: Keys to a Fulfilling Partnership*

"WOW. If you are the kind of person who 'feels' everything, then this book is a must read. I've personally worked with **Jean Haner** *with great results, and her magnificent book is a must-have if you want to create peace, harmony, and tranquility in your physical environments and your life."*

—**Nick Ortner**, *New York Times* best-selling author of *The Tapping Solution: A Revolutionary System for Stress-Free Living*

"What an engaging, practical, down-to-earth, and user-friendly guide we have here! **Jean Haner** *has masterfully succeeded in explaining what any person can do to clear, lighten up, and free the space we live in. I was intrigued by the real-life examples and simple yet authoritative explanations. If you are ready to clear, this manual will be your welcome friend!"*

—**Alan Cohen**, author of *A Deep Breath of Life: Daily Inspiration for Heart-Centered Living*

"In Clear Home, Clear Heart, Jean Haner has done an excellent job of addressing the powerful effect that energy has on our lives. Her new book offers a thorough understanding of how to identify and release the negative energy that causes distress in our environment, in our relationships, and to our emotional and physical health. As someone who lives life from an energetic perspective, I started using her strategies right away and feel deeply grateful for this practical handbook!"

—**Cheryl Richardson**, *New York Times* best-selling author of *The Art of Extreme Self Care*

"We all desire excellent health and happy homes, and most of us put regular effort into creating both. But sometimes we fall short of our goals for no apparent reason. Why isn't the diet working? Why do we always fight in the same room? Why do we repeat the same pattern again and again? In her new book, Clear Home, Clear Heart, Jean Haner explains that stuck energy could be the culprit and offers easy ways to address it using the ancient Chinese Five Elements. Engaging and to the point, I strongly recommend this book as a must-read for anyone interested in improving their health, environment, and life in general."

—**Vicki Matthews**, author/blogger at Ask Vicki:
Relationship Remedies Using the Five Elements

"Jean Haner has a rare gift of linking the practical and the sacred. She opens up a world and guides us effortlessly through it. The information in Clear Home, Clear Heart is inspiring, empowering and accessible; the techniques are life changing."

—**Virginia Bell**, author of *Midlife Is Not a Crisis: Using Astrology to Thrive in the Second Half of Life*

"Jean Haner's book was refreshing in that up until now I've always considered clearing to be something that was done for me rather than by me. I didn't consider that I could learn this process and put it to use for myself and others. "Of particular interest to me is the connection Jean made to mindfulness and that one can learn to clear and immediately let go of the emotions or feelings that come up. I've recommended Jean's book to a friend who is extremely sensitive to other people's energy; it will be a wonderful tool in the development of her ability to cope with particularly toxic people as well as the day-to-day situations she finds herself in."

—**Susan Opeka**, founder and CEO of
The Present Moment, Inc.

CLEAR HOME
CLEAR HEART

also by JEAN HANER

BOOKS

The Wisdom of Your Face:
Change Your Life with Chinese Face Reading

The Wisdom of Your Child's Face:
Discover Your Child's True Nature with Chinese Face Reading!

Your Hidden Symmetry:
How Your Birth Date Reveals the Plan for Your Life

All of the above are available at your local bookstore,
or may be ordered by visiting:

Jean Haner: www.jeanhaner.com
Hay House USA: www.hayhouse.com®
Hay House Australia: www.hayhouse.com.au
Hay House UK: www.hayhouse.co.uk
Hay House South Africa: www.hayhouse.co.za
Hay House India: www.hayhouse.co.in

CLEAR HOME
CLEAR HEART

learn to clear

the energy

of people

& places

JEAN HANER

HAY HOUSE, INC.
Carlsbad, California • New York City
London • Sydney • Johannesburg
Vancouver • New Delhi

Published and distributed in the United States by: Hay House, Inc.:
www.hayhouse.com® • *Published and distributed in Australia by:*
Hay House Australia Pty. Ltd.: www.hayhouse.com.au • *Published and
distributed in the United Kingdom by:* Hay House UK, Ltd.: www.hay
house.co.uk • *Published and distributed in the Republic of South Africa by:* Hay House SA (Pty), Ltd.: www.hayhouse.co.za • *Distributed in
Canada by:* Raincoast Books: www.raincoast.com • *Published in India
by:* Hay House Publishers India: www.hayhouse.co.in

Project editor: Nicolette Salamanca Young
Cover design: Charles McStravick • *Interior design:* Riann Bender
Interior illustrations: Jeff Dong

Cataloging-in-Publication Data is
on file with the Library of Congress

ISBN: 978-1-4019-5154-2

10 9 8 7 6 5 4 3 2 1
1st edition, March 2017

Printed in the United States of America

For my father,
with deep gratitude

CONTENTS

Introduction xiii

PART I: PERSONAL CLEARING

Chapter 1: Canary in the Coal Mine .3

Chapter 2: And Then There's *You*:
The Part You Play in Creating Your Stress 15

Chapter 3: Learning to Clear Energy 25

Chapter 4: How to Clear Personal Energy Fields 37

Chapter 5: Continuing with the Personal Clearing:
The Inner Fields 61

Chapter 6: After the Clearing:
Advice, Answers & Reminders 91

PART II: SPACE CLEARING

Chapter 7: Emotions Can Linger in a Space. 111

Chapter 8: How to Clear the Residue of Emotions
Held in a Space 119

Chapter 9: How to Clear Geopathic Stress 141

Chapter 10: How to Clear Adverse Effects of Technology . . .157

Chapter 11: Final Stages of the Space Clearing 165

PART III: ACTIVATING THE POWER OF YOUR COMPASSIONATE HEART

Chapter 12: How and Why Does Clearing Work? 185

Chapter 13: Clearing: A New Approach to Mindfulness 195

Chapter 14: Stages of Learning. 207

Resources 221

Acknowledgments 223

About the Author 225

INTRODUCTION

By age 16, Alex was already very spiritual. He'd recently started waking up an hour earlier each day so he could meditate and do yoga in his room before breakfast. But something, he felt, was really *wrong* with him.

Every morning, after he finished his hour of meditation and yoga, he felt *wonderful*—clear, in balance, and full of joy. He'd then head out his bedroom door and down a long hallway through the house to the kitchen, where his mother had breakfast waiting. However, by the time he sat down at the kitchen table, all the joy was melting away. He would start feeling heavy and tired—and so upset with himself! What was going on with him that he couldn't hold that great feeling for more than five minutes?

But there was nothing "wrong" with Alex that made him unable to maintain the lovely state of mind he reached in his room each morning. It was just that he was being weighed down by the residue of negative emotions that filled the rest of the house. As he walked down that long, narrow hallway to the kitchen, he left behind the clear energy he'd created in his bedroom and immersed himself in the energy of his home. With each step, he was more and more affected by the invisible vibrations held in the house—of his father's stress, his mother's worries, his sister's teenage drama, his older brother's depression.

Every time you have a thought or feeling, it doesn't just evaporate into nothing. Instead, you make a little deposit of that energy into your environment. And over time, these deposits can gradually build up, like invisible house dust, to form a thick layer in the space. It's like an invisible cloud of whatever you've been feeling every time you pass there. If the feelings you're having are positive ones, those will accumulate and increase the possibility that every time you're there, you'll feel happy again. But if the thoughts or feelings are stressed or negative ones, those will build up as well, making it more likely that you'll continue to feel like *that* each time you're in that place.

For example, if you feel a moment of anxiety as you approach your front door to leave each morning, worrying if you've forgotten anything or nervous about what the day will bring, you leave a little imprint of that anxious feeling in that spot. And if, when you come back through the door each night, you heave a big sigh as you offload the stress from the day, that also makes a little deposit in that same area. If you do this day after day, month after month, then over time it accumulates and compounds. Then every time you walk through that spot, you're influenced by what's already hanging in that cloud, and you'll be more likely to have those feelings again. This can keep you locked into repetitive patterns of emotions without your even being aware of it.

In every environment, there's an energy held there from what the people in that space have experienced. Have you ever walked into a room where there's just been an argument and felt like the atmosphere was so thick you could cut it with a knife? Or have you ever entered a room and it just didn't feel right? You wanted to turn around and leave but you couldn't explain why? These are the same kinds of things.

Further, it's not just the leftover "stuff" in the places in which we spend time that is affecting us. The subtle energy of the people we're with each day also plays a huge part in influencing how we feel. Have you ever considered that one of the reasons you may feel so tired after a trip to the shopping mall or a day at the office is because you're worn out from having to deal with the energy of all those people around you?

We are open systems in constant communication with the invisible world around us. Our thoughts, emotions, and physiology are all far more affected than we realize by the subtle vibrations of the people we live and work with and the environments we move through. For the most part, this experience is a daily stressor for us—but it doesn't have to be that way! This book will show you what you can do when you encounter energy that's out of balance, whether it's from a person or a place. Rather than be negatively impacted, you can *clear* this energy, return it to a balanced and healthy state of flow, and prevent yourself from being stressed as well.

I used to be quite reticent about bringing up the subject of "energy" with people, especially the more skeptical, left-brained types—which I actually am as well! However, throughout my 30 years of study, research, and experience in working with the energy of people and environments, I've found that nearly everyone I speak with is actually thirsting for permission to talk about how they're affected by energy, and searching for some language to describe what's actually happening to them. This is why I feel this book is so necessary: to make this information more available to those who are yearning to deepen and develop their understanding of what's going on in the invisible world around them and how to cope in healthy ways.

Do You Leak Your Feelings?

It's not only the outside world (the people around us and the places we inhabit) that can affect our emotions and experiences. We have a whole inner world that can do so, and this energy can need clearing too.

For an example, let's look at my client Lisa. In her case, you could say she doesn't so much absorb energy as *leak* it. You can see the effects of this energy leak in the story of her week, which she described as "disaster after disaster!"

Lisa's seven-year-old son attended a weekly karate class with an instructor who had an extremely strict and critical teaching style. This man often spoke unkindly to the kids and was even rude to the parents. One day, he was particularly hard on her son and made him cry. After Lisa saw her son run out of the building, tears streaming down his face, and heard his story, she fell into a rage. She *hated* that man!

That night, Lisa seethed with anger as she stuffed her son's karate uniform into the washing machine, just anticipating having to take him to next week's class. Half an hour later, the washing machine broke down and flooded the laundry room floor.

A few days later, Lisa stopped by the karate school to pay the monthly bill. As she walked down the hallway to the office, she felt the emotions swelling up yet again and her blood pressure rising. When she returned to her parking spot, it rose even more as she discovered she had a flat tire!

Lisa's head pounded as she cooked dinner that evening. She was so upset about the karate teacher, the washing machine, and the flat tire. Could all that toxic emotion in her system have mixed into the stew as she stirred it? Because that night the whole family ended up with indigestion.

Lisa was leaking her angry feelings; in other words, she was creating a huge energetic charge that was broadcast from her system, and it affected everyone and everything around her. Sure, it could just be a coincidence that when she was so upset, things started going haywire around her, but I've seen this happen far too many times to think it was just chance.

How This Book Can Help You

We are both affecting and affected by the world around us all the time. If you're highly sensitive, it's likely you're already very familiar with the experience of being challenged by all that you feel in the energy around you. But in fact, as more and more people work on personal growth to expand their consciousness, they're becoming aware of energy in ways they hadn't been before, and looking for answers about how to manage their newfound sensitivity. At the same time, as they do their inner work and see that the weight of past experiences, and the tension they hold around their pain or difficulties, may be affecting their current life, they're looking for ways to let all that go.

This book will teach you how to clear your own energy so you can release your past, or move beyond your stuck places, and become a creative force in your life again. It will teach you how to clear other people, to open a more spacious and harmonious place for them to be in their own lives. You will also learn how to clear the energy of all the spaces you live in, whether long-term such as your home and workplace, or short-term like your hotel room or airplane seat! There are three parts to this book:

— Part I will explain the ways in which we are amazing receivers and transmitters of energy as we walk through the world. You'll learn more about how your thoughts and feelings are affected by those around you and how you also broadcast your own inner story in ways that can cause yourself and others stress. You will learn step-by-step techniques to clear the energy of any living being, whether it's yourself, a friend, your client, or your puppy! This section also offers practical guidance concerning the experience of giving and receiving clearings.

— In Part II, we'll look at how the energy of your surroundings affects you and how you can clear all the spaces you inhabit. You'll learn how to release stagnant energy and the residue of emotions from a place, whether that's an imbalance left from a fight with your boyfriend last week or some feelings stuck in the space from a previous occupant's unhappiness there decades before.

You'll then discover how the energy of the earth can impact how you feel in your home or office. The earth has meridians of energy that run through it, much like in your own body. When a person's energy (*qi*) becomes imbalanced, they might see an acupuncturist.* In a similar

---

* In this book, in order to avoid awkward "he/she" or "him/her" references, I prefer to use the neutral pronoun "they." Interestingly, this was an accepted universal pronoun in the English language as early as the times of Chaucer, used for masculine and feminine, singular and plural. This fell out of favor in the 18th century, when the new rule was that "he" should be used for both men and women, and that certainly doesn't seem to fit our times.

fashion, we can work with the life-force of the earth to bring back balance and flow.

You'll also learn about the impact of all our wonderful technology and how to ease stress on your system from things like electromagnetic fields or microwave radiation. This section concludes by walking you through a space clearing from beginning to end, so you know exactly what to do to create a home filled with vibrant, healthy energy!

— Part III takes you even deeper into your understanding of what's really happening during a clearing. You'll see how, in the process of learning how to clear energy, you're actually transforming yourself as well. As you practice clearing, you're simultaneously changing *who you are* within yourself, and radically transforming how you relate to any experience you encounter. This is a training that can revolutionize the rest of your life.

You've Come to the Right Place

Several years ago, I was in the waiting room of a radio studio, about to go on the air to be interviewed about my work with energy clearing. The author who was scheduled to go on after me arrived all frazzled, having had a really tough day. When she found out what I was going to be talking about, she said, "Oh god, would you mind—could you possibly do a clearing for me right now?"

For a split second, I thought, *Sheesh, I'm trying to get focused for my interview!* But then I realized how silly that was: doing a clearing benefits my own energy as well, so it could only make my interview go better! I sat with her and cleared for a few minutes, and then we quickly exchanged hugs and business cards as I headed into the studio.

A few hours later, I got an e-mail from her: "WOW! In those 10 minutes of clearing, I lost an emotional 20 pounds! WHERE DO I LEARN HOW TO DO THIS STUFF?!?!"

Well, if this is how you're starting to feel, you've come to the right place. Here's where you can learn it. Let's start from the beginning . . .

part I

PERSONAL
CLEARING

🪷 🪷 🪷

Healing may not be so much about getting better,
as about letting go of everything that isn't you—
all of the expectations, all of the beliefs—
and becoming who you are.

— Rachel Naomi Remen

chapter 1

Canary
in the Coal Mine

I was born "wide open." As a child, I could physically feel the invisible energy of people, places, and even objects. Sometimes this was fun. For instance, if my mother lost her keys, I would walk around the house, feeling the air with my hand until I felt a little "zotz" in my palm. Then, invariably, I'd look down to discover the missing keys in that very spot, under the stack of mail or in between the couch cushions.

I loved to "taste" the energy of the different places in my house. I'd sit in my father's chair in the living room and feel his essence, and then run upstairs to immerse myself in the atmosphere of my big sister's room and how it felt to be a teenager. But there was a significant downside to this kind of sensitivity. I could walk into an empty room and feel the emotions held there from an argument that had happened weeks ago. I'd start to feel sick, overwhelmed from absorbing the intensity of that information. So you can imagine how I felt at school each day, surrounded by the cacophony of energy from all the kids in my classroom—and even the entire building. I was sick throughout my childhood because I was a little sponge, soaking in, and being affected by, all the energy around me.

When my parents took me to visit a family friend at the hospital, I nearly fainted from the overwhelm of sensing all the energy of illness, stress, and anxiety filling that building. After five minutes, they had to rush me outside. They assumed I was frightened by being in a hospital for the first time, and I certainly couldn't explain to them what was really going on. I knew no words to describe the experience of being an empath. (Most people now refer to this as being a "highly sensitive person," and psychologists believe that this includes at least 20 percent of the population.) At the time, I just thought that there was something terribly wrong with me. It wasn't until I was in my 20s that I started getting clues that this might not be some personal failing on my part after all—that it might actually have to do with something real.

Hmmm—Maybe I'm Not Crazy After All!

When I married into a Chinese family, my very traditional mother-in-law insisted on being part of the hunt for our first house. But she had some rather strange rules about which houses were acceptable, all part of what she called "fung sooey." This was 15 years before feng shui (usually pronounced "fung shway," the ancient Chinese science of how our environment affects us) became known in the United States, so I had no idea what she was talking about, but I *did* pay attention. What she was saying was a revelation to me. Could it be that there really was an invisible energy in houses that could affect us? Maybe I wasn't crazy after all!

I began to experiment as we looked at houses for sale. I'd walk through the rooms and hold my hand a few inches away from the walls, trying to read the information in each environment. I found that I could identify where stagnant energy was held in a space. Slight stuckness felt like I was brushing cobwebs; thicker stagnation felt like I was running my hand through mud. When I reached a place where someone had felt some strong emotions, it was like walking into an invisible curtain. I could even sense where the electrical wiring was running inside the walls.

My mother-in-law became my first feng shui teacher, but I went on to ravenously study with every teacher I could find. After several years, I was practicing feng shui professionally. But I soon found that I was less interested in the "visibles," such as where to put the couch or what color the wallpaper should be, and much more interested in the "invisibles"—the stagnant or stressed energy I felt in a space that was affecting the people there. After all, even if the placement for the couch is visually "correct" according to feng shui principles, if it's in a spot that holds disturbed energy from a bad argument, then no one is going to feel good sitting there!

As I walked through a house during one consultation, I felt intense resentment radiating from a beautiful clock on the wall. My client noticed me pause there and said, "Oh, yeah, that clock hung in my office for the twenty years I was a bookkeeper. *God*, I hated that job!" So there on her wall sat that clock, each day broadcasting messages of what it had absorbed during all her unhappy years of work. It wasn't just a visual reminder; after all, I could *feel* it, and I'd had no knowledge of the clock's history. Every time she passed by, it would trigger negativity, below the level of her consciousness, but still impacting her mood on a daily basis.

I had a similar experience in the new home of a just-divorced man. His bedroom was lovely, but when I stood next to the bed, I sensed frustration. I heard angry voices and my jaw began to ache. "How old is your mattress?" I asked.

"Oh wow," he replied. "It's got to be at least twelve years old; my ex and I bought it when we got married."

"Did you two argue before you went to sleep at night?"

"Hell, yes," he said. "I think that's what made me start grinding my teeth when I slept. And I still do."

Ah, so that's why my jaw hurt: I was sensing what his own system had done over the years that got imprinted in the bedding. I explained that his mattress was keeping him immersed in the accumulated frustration and anger that he and his ex-wife felt during all those years of arguments in bed as their marriage came to a painful end.

He suddenly realized that he and his new girlfriend had started arguing as *they* lay in bed trying to get to sleep; the old energy was affecting his new relationship! "I'm buying a new mattress *today*," he said, looking at his watch. It could get pretty expensive for my clients, I worried, if I kept finding furnishings that had to be replaced because they held negative energy!

Of course, there were positive sensations too. I felt pure sweetness radiating out of an antique dresser that had been inherited from a loving grandmother, and I sensed the layers of contentment that had soaked into a rocking chair from generations of mothers watching their babies asleep in their arms. These things broadcast out healthy, loving messages into the environment and supported the happiness of everyone there.

The more I worked, the more I refined my skills at sensing energy and interpreting what I was feeling. When I first walked into a house, I was able to tell immediately if someone there had recently been ill. I found that I could run my hand above a woman's bed and know if she were pregnant. I would hover my hand above her husband's pillow and recognize what he worried about as he tried to fall asleep at night. People started calling me the House Psychic!

I was opening to energy more and more, and it was fascinating. But I really had no idea what I was doing, and I was starting to wade into deep water without having learned how to swim.

Uh-oh—Maybe I Need to Rethink This

After each feng shui consultation, I was entirely depleted because I was taking on the energy I encountered. My clients felt much better, but I felt much worse! I had no business continuing this practice without knowing how to better manage the energy. This was driven home to me the night I went into labor for someone else.

At the time, I had two feng shui clients: one was a midwife and the other was her patient, who had just discovered she was pregnant. They asked me if they could call me to let me know when the one went into labor so I might energetically support the birth process and help things go as easily as possible. "Sure, I'd be honored!" I said. I didn't really know what that might entail since this had nothing to do with feng shui, but I imagined that I'd send them both love and light once I got the call.

7

Well, months went by, and we didn't really keep in touch. In fact, I only rarely thought of our conversation. Then, at 7:30 one night, I suddenly doubled over in extreme pain. It felt as though my uterus was exploding, and I was gasping for breath. I tried everything I could think of to alleviate the pain, but nothing was working. What was going on? Obviously something was seriously wrong with me, so at 10:30, I put on my coat to go to the emergency room. Just as suddenly, my pain vanished. Puzzled and shaky, I fell into bed, just grateful that I seemed to be all right again.

The next morning, my phone rang. It was the midwife! She told me that her patient had gone into labor the previous afternoon, but things had taken a sudden and drastic bad turn. (This was in the days before cell phones, so they had no chance to call me.) She said, "We were both in the hospital room, just calling out your name." Sometime around 7 P.M., the woman started experiencing extreme pain, but she was set on a natural, drug-free birth and refused any help to ease things. After about three hours, she finally allowed them to administer an epidural, which took effect at—you guessed it—10:30. Her pain disappeared, and she gave birth to a healthy baby boy soon after.

What had happened? Well, we had made the agreement months before. My system knew I was to be available, and so, below the level of my awareness, I picked up the signal as they both cried out for my help. Unconsciously, I then did the only thing I knew how to do: soak up energy. I tried to relieve her pain by taking it on myself—*not* the right way to handle things! We are not meant to help someone by moving suffering from their body to our own.

It was already difficult enough for me to move through the world in everyday life, being affected by the energy of everything around me and not knowing how to have good boundaries. And now I was trying to let go of all boundaries to open up *more?* Crazy!

Chastened, I embarked on a journey to try to change what was such an overwhelming challenge for me into something that was at least manageable. But what actually occurred would revolutionize my entire life.

Whoosh—The Clearing Happened!

I studied everything I could find about energy work and specifically space clearing as practiced for centuries in cultures all over the world. I learned about crude techniques like making loud noises to break up stuck energy, smudging with sage, burying "power" objects in the ground, and walking around the house clockwise or counterclockwise depending on what you wanted the result to be. A Chinese qi gong master even taught me the secrets of how to move negative energies from important parts of the house and embed them into a doorframe to keep them contained, where they wouldn't cause so much trouble!

My studies then took me to intensive training with powerful teachers that extended over years of time. I learned methods that involved very precise and elaborate procedures to clear the energy of an environment and bring back balance. The teachings were firm: if you performed all the steps exactly—in the correct way, in the proper order, and at the right time—then the clearing would be successful.

And it worked. Because I could feel energy, I could tell when the clearing happened. I would feel a sudden *whoosh*, and there would be an amazing shift to a beautiful, pristine, almost crystalline clarity filling the house.

Sometimes at that point, the sun would even come out and flood the space with light. Or I might hear.my client say, "I don't know what you're doing, but just now I started feeling so much better!"

However, something was going wrong. I quickly began to notice the *whoosh* of the clearing happening earlier and earlier in the session, long before I'd completed all the steps. I'd be halfway through the process, and I'd feel the change happen. Then it got *worse*. I started feeling the clearing happen as I pushed the doorbell when I first arrived at the house! Later, I'd just pull up in my car, park in front of the house—*whoosh*.

It got to the point that I felt the energy shift *while still on the phone* with a client who'd called to make an appointment for a space clearing. In fact, I was afraid that they might call back the next day to say, "You know, I don't think I really need this after all. Things here are suddenly better." I'd want to say, "Wait—let me send you a bill!"

What was going on? I realized that the clearing wasn't actually dependent on the complex ceremony I performed or the special objects I placed to change the energy. What had happened was that in the process of learning to clear, *I'd* changed. My system had been trained to respond to energy in a new way. Now, when I encountered stress held in a space, it would transform just through my conscious connection, as a result of the level of heart-based awareness I'd learned to hold.

The truth is, it's actually not about what you *do*; it's really about who you *are*. The power is not in the "doing"; it's in the "being"—and I had learned how to "be" in a whole new way. (As you read this book, you're also on that same journey, one that can change your life in ways you may not yet even be imagining.)

So it wasn't just my clients who were benefiting; the more clearings I did, the more peaceful I became in my own life. The clearings were like an even more advanced training for me in how to relate to all the energy I encountered, even within my daily experience. I no longer needed hours alone to recover from spending time in crowded places. I found that I was now recognizing the moment I started to take on other people's stress and automatically clearing it before it could take hold in my system.

The things I used to hold a personal charge around, big or little, started to melt away. That old experience in the past that had continued to cause me pain for years? Now, it was like: *Huh. What was all the fuss about?* The memory of the event was still there, of course, but my difficult feelings about it had disappeared. Through the process of learning how to ease stress for other people, I'd learned to do it for myself as well.

As I went on to develop this work, what evolved was more than a way to teach how to bring the energy of both people and places into balance; it was an elegant training for how to walk through your own life, centered and at peace, with your heart able to dance with whatever or whomever you encountered. This aspect led a prominent meditation teacher who came to one of my workshops to call clearing "accelerated meditation." She didn't mean it in terms of "get enlightenment quick!" She believed that clearing brought people to a place of calm and joyful open-heartedness within weeks or months instead of the years that a meditation practice would need to achieve the same result.

Entrainment: You Synchronize to the Energy around You

We're all affected by the subtle energy around us, though it often happens below the level of our consciousness. Real estate agents talk about people who walk onto the porch of a house with great curb appeal but turn around and walk away before they even reach the front door. On some level they sense the energy isn't right. You may have had the experience of thinking of a friend moments before they e-mailed you, or hearing a text message arrive and knowing who had sent it before even looking. Biologist Rupert Sheldrake's book *The Sense of Being Stared At* shares fascinating studies proving that we often can feel it if someone is staring at us, even when they're standing behind us.

We all are amazingly sensitive receivers of the invisible information around us. With my hypersensitivity, I was like the canary in the coal mine, experiencing symptoms and feeling the energy in ways other people wouldn't. (But remember, if the canary goes into the coal mine and keels over—that means it's not okay for anyone to be there!) Some people are highly aware and struggle to manage that experience. Others keep themselves so distracted that they don't notice that they're being affected. And for all of us, it's natural to assume that the thoughts or feelings we're having are ours, rather than coming from the person sitting next to us in Starbucks!

Research has shown that in restaurants, people tend to chew their food to the speed of the music playing in the background. *That's not about sensing energy,* you might be thinking. *It's just about hearing, one of our regular five senses. It's probably that they're listening to the beat of the music and unconsciously aligning to it.* Well, scientists also found that if there's no music playing, and even if someone's sitting at the table eating alone, they will tend to chew to the same speed of those eating around them. Now, we can be pretty sure people aren't looking around to see how fast others are chewing and trying to match their rhythm!

Researchers have even found that people react to the subtle background hum of the electrical current in their environment. In the U.S. and Canada, electricity operates at a current of 60 cycles per second. The resonant frequency of that kind of electrical current relates to the B natural tone on a musical scale. In Europe, the electrical current is 50 cycles per second, which relates to G sharp on a musical scale. In one study, a group of students from the U.S., Canada, and Germany were asked to spontaneously hum whatever tone came to mind. For the North Americans, B natural was the most frequent one hummed. As for the Germans? They hummed G sharp.

What's going on? We're not just affected by the invisible world around us; we actually *synchronize* with it. In science, the concept is called "entrainment," which is when separate systems come into a coherent rhythm with one another. This principle can be demonstrated if you put a bunch of grandfather clocks in a room together, each with their pendulum swinging at a different rate from the others. After some time, you'd come back to find that all the pendulums were now swinging in unison, their rhythms entrained. This is the same reason many people report that studying in person with a guru is so powerful for their spiritual development—just sitting in the presence of the guru entrains their system to hold a different vibration.

The unfortunate fact is that most of us aren't hanging out with gurus in our everyday lives. Instead, *we're* surrounded by co-workers—some who may have just had a fight with their husband, or who got only three hours of sleep last night, or who are freaking out about that big deadline—all broadcasting their feelings out into their environment! Your system can entrain to that stress, and it can stay with you, affecting how you think and feel throughout the day. It can be held in your energy field, so when you come home in the evening, you're walking in the door not only with your own stress but also what you took on from others as well.

My client Stephanie discovered how this was happening in her own life. Her husband worked in a busy urban hospital emergency room, and when his shift ended in the middle of the night, he'd crawl into bed while she was already fast asleep. No matter how quietly he eased himself onto the mattress, she'd immediately wake up. Stephanie said, "I just get this awful feeling. It's not from him, but more like it's from a big cloud *around* him. It makes me so uncomfortable, I can't relax and go back to sleep." What this highly sensitive woman was experiencing was not just how her husband felt after finishing his work that night. It was also all the anxiety and panic of the patients, the stress of the medical staff, and probably even the intense effects of all the electromagnetic fields from the equipment in the hospital that had infiltrated her husband's energy field and followed him home to bed.

You may already be able to identify experiences in your own life where you feel as though you were affected by other people's energy or by the environment you were living in. We are always receiving "information" from the world around us that impacts us in different ways. But it's important to understand that's not the whole picture. We're receivers of energy—but we're transmitters too! And that's what we need to discuss next.

chapter 2

And Then There's *You*

---

the part you play in creating your stress

An important concept in understanding this work is the part you play in creating stress and imbalance for *yourself.* Scientists say that as much as 93 percent of our thoughts are the same from one day to the next! Who we are is very much based on a story we keep telling ourselves over and over.

When you first arrive here as a baby, your energy is clear and your mind hasn't yet become stuck in some repetitive story. You may bring with you some issues you've inherited in your DNA, but for the most part, your body, mind, and spirit are relatively balanced. But then you start to have experiences. Some of them are pleasant and positive, and so you process them easily. Some, however, are intense or uncomfortable, and you're not able to integrate them so well. Instead, they can be held in your energy field as unloved parts of yourself, what psychiatrist Carl Jung called your *shadow*. These memories and feelings can become like a thick filter through which you view the world, subtly influencing your reactions in every moment.

Another way to understand how we can get locked into certain ways of being was expressed by scientist John Dove Isaacs in his book with Daniel Behrman, *John Isaacs and His Oceans*: "There is no tyranny so profound as the tyranny of the first successful solution." When you are a vulnerable child and encounter your first real challenge, you will eventually come up with some solution that *does* work, which helps you survive that stressful event. Thank goodness, you found a life preserver in a situation where you didn't know how to cope. The problem is when that successful solution becomes an ongoing strategy, one that you keep relying on even when it's not valid or useful for new problems. When you use this strategy inappropriately and ineffectively, it can even cause additional suffering and more opportunities for adding to your shadow.

These accumulated "unloved" experiences from your past are held in your energy: what your mother said to you in anger when you were two, the unkind treatment by a teacher in third grade, your big romantic breakup in adolescence, the critical boss you had last year, the aggressive driver who cut you off on the freeway this morning. Do you remember the character Pig-Pen from the *Peanuts* cartoons, the one who always walked around immersed in a cloud of dirt and dust? That's actually what most people look like to me because they're carrying the stress they've taken on from the world around them as well as the negativity they continue to create and project from their inner world.

We're often told to imagine ourselves as "beings of light"; instead, to one degree or other, we're all actually walking around surrounded by a fog of stuff stuck in our energy fields that blocks our radiance from shining through. If we were covered in grime and dust, we wouldn't think of skipping a shower before leaving the house. Yet we go out each day covered in the energetic gunk of yesterday—well, really, the last 20, 30, 40, or however many years!

So we've learned that the stress from your life experiences can linger in your energy and affect you from that point forward. And the more tension you hold around those feelings, the more they can weigh you down or create blocks in your system. This can eventually form an energetic vibration that attracts more of the same. The result can be that you keep dating the same kind of person even though you think you're making different choices each time, or moving to get away from a noisy apartment only to end up with loud neighbors yet again! You can end up feeling stuck in life, dealing with an ongoing fatigue that never seems to resolve, or being too limited in how you view yourself and your choices.

Jung's psychotherapeutic techniques are based on the belief that if you can bring your shadow personality into awareness and integrate it, this will eliminate its negative effects and release positive energy that had previously been trapped. Jung said, "One does not become enlightened by imagining figures of light, but by making the darkness conscious. The latter procedure, however, is disagreeable and therefore not popular." His dry humor in that statement always makes me smile. However, as our understanding of consciousness and subtle energy has been refined, many now suggest that it's not necessary to dredge up and relive past trauma in order to assimilate it.

This stress wasn't a part of you when you first arrived, and it doesn't have to be a part of you any longer. It's just energy, and it can be cleared. It may happen after only one clearing or it may take several clearings, each one slowly taking the charge out of something you've been holding on to, until all of a sudden you realize, *poof*, it's gone! What used to stress you no longer has any power over you.

Sometimes people ask me where the "bad" energy goes during a clearing. They're afraid that perhaps it's going to leap off them and then get stuck on someone else! But this isn't about "bad" or "good" anything. It's really about releasing stuck energy so there can be a healthy flow again. An easy way to understand what happens during a clearing is to imagine a garden hose with a kink in it. The kink in the hose prevents the water from flowing out. If you unkink the hose, then the water flows freely. But where did the kink go? There was nothing there to "go" anywhere. Just as with the hose, if there's a knotted, stressed area in your system, then your energy, your emotions, and your physical qi get blocked. If we release the kink, ahhh, nice flow again.

Dobermans or Chihuahuas: Your Reactions to Your Experiences

Several years ago, right before his book *Blink* came out, I had the joy of sitting across from author Malcolm Gladwell at dinner and listening to him tell stories about his research for the book. One thing he'd done was interview people who train professional bodyguards. He said that as part of the training to become a bodyguard, each person is shown a line drawn on the ground and told, "Walk along this line, and no matter what happens, stay on the line."

As the trainee starts to walk along the line, from out of nowhere a snarling attack dog charges right at them! Of course, they shriek and run off the line. Then they realize that the dog is on a leash that restrains the animal just inches away from the line. So the student restarts their walk, and the attack dog comes back again—but this time, the dog is *off the leash*. At this point in the exercise, when the dog leaps on the trainee, the person basically loses all control in total terror! Then the trainee sees that the dog is muzzled and cannot hurt them. This training goes on and on, with different stress-inducing experiences, until the student can have anything happen and still they stay there, walking the line, in balance and unstressed.

I think this is an apt analogy—albeit an extreme one, for sure!—for what *we* do, how *we* respond to our everyday life experiences. When something happens to us, we have an immediate reaction, mentally, emotionally, and physically.

When you have an emotion, your body responds, and your system is flooded with all kinds of juicy little messengers that change your physiology. These can be wonderful changes that lift your spirits for the rest of the day if, for instance, you gaze into the face of a little baby. But you can also have daily experiences that aren't so positive: you make a mistake at work, or your spouse gets upset with you, or some idiot cuts you off in traffic. In these cases, it's like encountering those attack dogs in Malcolm's story, and when your system goes into reaction, you can get knocked off-balance on all levels. It can take you mere moments to recover, or it can continue negatively rocking your world for the rest of your day.

In some cases, there can be bigger upsets that affect you for years. The shock waves in your system from being raised by an emotionally volatile parent or having your heart shattered by an unfaithful lover, for example, can keep you locked into patterns of stress and imbalance in subtle ways you don't even recognize. It's when you start to do inner work, devoting time to personal growth and spiritual development, that you come to see how the weight of past experiences, and the charge you hold around old pain or difficulties, affects how you respond to your current life experiences, and you start searching for ways to let all that go.

You shouldn't underestimate the small upsets during your day. Even if you recover from them in a few moments, they still matter. Although they may not be attack dogs— they may be little Chihuahuas!—they can have a cumulative effect, creating an ongoing undercurrent of stress so you're never feeling quite in balance.

And the deeper upsets? These are the encounters with the Dobermans of stress, the traumas that are severe enough to get stored in your energy fields even after a one-time experience. They can keep you locked into projecting old reactions onto your new experiences, preventing you from moving forward with your life's purpose and finding true happiness.

Walk Your Line

To one degree or another, we're all walking around carrying stress from people, places, or events in our past. We're also in constant reaction to our current experiences. To break this cycle so that you can walk your own personal "line" without falling off and to be a creative force in your life again, there are two abilities you need to learn:

1. Release the old stuck energy

2. Transform how you react to new stress

The first ability is what you learn with clearing: releasing the old stuff. In my clearing workshops, what I often see as I look at the group seems like steam rising from each person! It's all the old energy getting set free as people let go of things they've been carrying in their fields for years, even decades.

Then the second ability comes as you continue to give and receive clearings. You suddenly realize that things have mysteriously changed; you're responding to your life from an elegant place of harmony and balance no matter what happens. If something stressful occurs, you just clear yourself and the stress moves on! And more and more, you won't even have to do any clearing for yourself. You'll maintain a state of consciousness where things rarely stress you, so there's less and less of a need to clear.

Transformations will affect every aspect of your life, happening gradually over time—or even instantaneously. Marie, a gregarious community organizer in her 40s, e-mailed after attending a clearing workshop: "I've never been able to read a thing without my glasses, and I owned several pairs, keeping them at work, at my bedside, in my car, around the house, because I was helpless without them. Well, two weeks after the clearing retreat, someone at my office asked me when I'd gotten contacts. And that's when I finally realized I'd taken off my glasses at some point during the workshop and never put them back on again. My eyesight is perfect!"

Where Clearing Can Take Us

So far, we've talked about how we're constantly influenced by the energy around us. Yes, we're often negatively impacted by all the stressed people around us and the stuck energy held in the spaces in which we live and work. But wait—it works both ways! That means the opposite is true as well—we can turn this around to be positively influenced instead! So before we get on with actually learning how to do a clearing, I need to tell you one final story, as an example of this.

Many years ago, my dear friend Marianne was dying of breast cancer. She had actually survived with it for 10 years, trying everything that both alternative medicine and Western medicine offered. But nothing had worked, and finally she was coming to the end of her life. As she prepared for the passage, I planned to be available for her.

This is one of the things I do with clearing: support people in the death process, working with the energy of their transition so there is as much ease as possible. With clearing, you don't have to be physically present with someone; since it can be done at a distance, I can tune in no matter where they are. In these situations, I often find that about three days before a person actually passes, I sense them entering a new phase. To me, it feels as if they've entered a dark wind tunnel, and they seem a bit disoriented and unsure. At that point, I will stay very connected and focused on clearing them to help with the process, and I often experience their relaxing into this stage more easily.

The evening came when I got an e-mail that Marianne was entering the final phases of dying and that it probably wouldn't be long now. I went into full clearing mode to be with her remotely, and I soon felt her step into that place that felt to me like the dark wind tunnel. I went to bed that night still energetically connected, expecting my usual experience of clearing over the next few days before finally feeling her pass.

But that's not what happened. Instead, I woke up the next morning in a complete and total state of bliss. It's nearly impossible to find words to describe the quality of what I was feeling. It's as close as I can imagine to the pure peace and joy of enlightenment. I went through the next three days, doing my regular work, buying groceries, cleaning the house, all the usual activities. But I did it all in a place of what felt like serene elation, even though that might sound like an improbable mix of feelings. This had never before been any part of my experience while clearing someone as they were dying.

It took me a while to figure out what was going on. Marianne had been friends with several spiritual teachers and healers around the world, and I'd known that I wasn't the only one connected energetically to her in this way. This was a group of highly advanced energy workers, each one tuning in to her remotely with their own particular form of support. So as I connected with her energy, I joined with their presence as well. I was benefitting from the network that had been formed by us all directing our conscious intention to the same place. I was uploading and downloading bliss.

But when I woke up on the third morning, the feelings had all faded away. I felt "normal" again, the elation gone. I checked my e-mail, and there it was, the message telling me Marianne had passed while I was asleep. Her spirit was gone, so the energetic network was no longer needed; it collapsed and our connection faded away.

Here we see where clearing can take us. Just as we are so negatively challenged and stressed by the transmissions

23

we receive from those around us, the opposite is also true. When people join together with the intent to bring balance, the same kind of energy transfer takes place between them in a positive way. Their systems synchronize; their bodies, minds, and hearts entrain; there is an energetic exchange stimulating each toward joy and peace.

When you learn how to do clearing, you can walk through the world as a fully compassionate presence and change the energy within you and around you. And when you need help, you can access a community of like minds who can clear *you*. There are people all around the world who've learned how to do this work, and many have come together online to be available for one another in this way.

In my workshops, I often say that I studied 30 years so I can teach this to you in four days. Now I can say that those 30 years have been compiled into these 248 pages, so you can learn this very simple, elegant, honoring way of activating the power of your compassionate heart. So let's get going.

chapter 3

Learning to Clear Energy

C learing is a subtle, gentle way to release the things that have been holding you back, to create infinite new possibilities for vitality and joy in life and connect you to your sacred sense of purpose. People often report feeling immediate shifts in their energy during a clearing, and that significant change unfolds in the days and weeks afterward, often in astonishing ways.

There is a tool to use when you do a clearing that can keep your analytical mind from overriding your ability to connect to someone's energy, help you stay focused, and let you know when each stage in the process is complete: a pendulum. Now, a pendulum is not some magical object with mysterious powers! It's basically just a weight on a string.

A pendulum

Pendulums have actually been used for hundreds, if not thousands, of years, all over the world. One of the age-old ways to use a pendulum was to determine whether a pregnant woman was going to have a girl or a boy. A needle hung from a string would be swung over her belly. If it swung one direction, the baby was predicted to be a boy; if it swung another way, then the baby would be a girl. That may or may not be folklore, but it does demonstrate one way that we can use the pendulum: interpreting its movement for "yes" or "no" answers.

First, of course, you'll need to acquire your own pendulum in order to learn how to get those answers! You can find pendulums in many spiritual bookstores, and there are plenty of online sources as well. (See the Resources in the back of this book.)

You can also make your own pendulum if you'd like. It can be as simple as a small rock tied to a length of yarn, or a heavy bead hung from a string or chain. If you make your own pendulum, follow these three basic guidelines:

1. The pendulum must be able to swing smoothly and freely in a circle, without

jerking or getting caught on the knot in the string or the attachment to the chain. Sometimes people try to use a necklace or key ring as a pendulum, but these often have a jerky motion to their swing because of how the pendant is connected to the chain or the key to the ring, and therefore are not good solutions.

2. The string or chain should be three or four inches in length. Any longer or shorter than that will affect ease of use and prevent you from getting accurate answers.

3. For the stone or bead or whatever you use for the weight, heavier is better. When you're just beginning to learn to use a pendulum, it's best if you can really feel that weight. If the pendulum is too light, it'll be hard to learn to "drive" it at first.

If you want to start immediately without buying or making a pendulum, you can simply use a wet tea bag! A dry one would be too light to use, but a wet one is heavy enough to work perfectly well. Just be sure to wring it out a bit before you use it, or it might spray a stain onto your shirt as it spins!

How to Hold Your Pendulum

Once you have your pendulum, hold it between your thumb and index finger. Most people hold the pendulum in the same hand they write with, but you can experiment to see what's most comfortable for you.

Keep your arm, wrist, and hand relaxed. When you're first learning to use a pendulum, it's normal to tense up and try too hard. Slightly bend your elbow and wrist, and hold the pendulum firmly, but don't clench it tightly between your fingers. Just let it dangle!

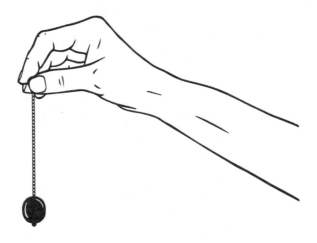

How to hold a pendulum

Give the pendulum a little swing, just to get a sense of how it feels to use one. Make friends with your pendulum—you're going to be using it a lot from now on! (For more detail, you can also view a video about how to use a pendulum at www.jeanhaner.com/clearingvideos.)

Finding Your "Yes" and "No"

There are four steps in learning how to use your pendulum to get "yes" and "no" answers to questions.

1. Pick up your pendulum and hold it a few inches above the palm of your other hand.

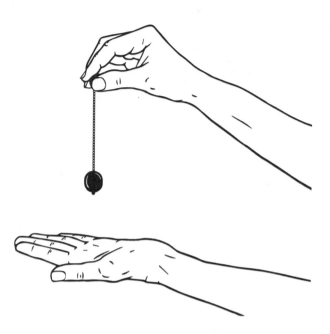

Step 1: Hold the pendulum over your palm.

Give it a little swing to get it moving, and then watch for a minute or two. You should see it gradually settle into a certain kind of regular movement as you hold it over your palm. For instance, it may swing in circles or side to side in a straight line. There is no right or wrong; everyone's pendulum will have its own kind of motion here.

2. Now you know what kind of movement the pendulum naturally makes when you hold it over the palm of your hand. While the pendulum is still swinging, flip your free hand over so that the pendulum is above the back of your hand.

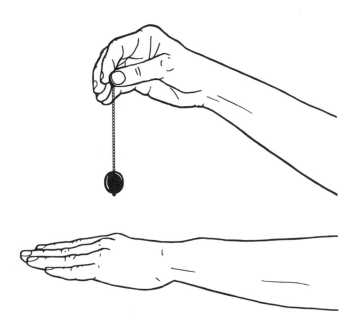

Step 2: Hold the pendulum over the back of your hand.

Observe what the pendulum does now. After a few moments, you will probably notice that the pendulum changes its movement! It swings in a different way over the back of your hand than it did over your palm. Again, it can be any kind of motion, circular, side to side, up and down. Just notice what it does for you. Remember that movement; it's the one the pendulum will consistently make when held over the back of your hand.

What's going on? Your body has a natural electromagnetic field that has a negative and a positive polarity. One side of your hand is the negative and one is the positive, and the pendulum is just reacting to that energy. You can try the same experiment by holding the pendulum over one knee to see how it swings, and then hold it over your other knee to notice it swing in a different way. The pendulum is really like a little biofeedback tool for you!

3. Hold the pendulum up in the air in the same relaxed way, but *without* your other hand beneath it.

Step 3: Hold the pendulum without your other hand beneath it.

Give the pendulum a little swing to get it moving. As it's moving, say, "Show me the movement for my 'yes.'" Soon it will settle into one of the motions that it had previously made, either the one over your palm or the one over the back of your hand.

Now you know what movement indicates that the answer to any question you're asking is "yes."

4. While the pendulum is still swinging, say, "Show me the movement for my 'no.'" Now watch as the pendulum begins to change how it moves! It will settle into the other motion it made previously, either the one over the palm or the one over the back of your hand.

Now you can use a pendulum to ask yes or no questions. You know which movement means the answer to your question is "yes" and which indicates a "no." Don't worry about what kinds of motion the pendulum makes. As long as the two swings are recognizably different, you're fine.

What to Do If You Don't Get Two Different Movements

What if the pendulum doesn't change its movement when you flip your hand? Maybe you see it swing in a circle over your palm, and when you turn your hand over, the pendulum *still* swings in a circle. This usually just means you're trying too hard! This is normal when we're learning something new.

It's important to be in a relaxed state of mind when you use a pendulum. So try taking a nice deep breath, have a sip of water, look out the window for a few moments, and then try again. Don't overthink it; just give the pendulum a few minutes to find its movement. Often, that's all it takes.

If the pendulum still makes the same motion above the palm and the back of your hand, try sitting in a different chair. Perhaps you were sitting in an area of stressed energy! If the pendulum *still* doesn't change movement, it's not a problem. All you have to do is assign yourself two different motions of your choice.

For example, you could hold the pendulum over your palm and make it swing in a circle, intending that *this* is your correct movement for when it's above your palm. Then hold it over the back of your hand and swing it side to side in straight lines. Tell yourself that *this* is now your correct motion for over the back of your hand.

Then, hold the pendulum up in the air (without your other hand beneath it), swing it in a circle, and say, "This is my 'yes.'" Now swing the pendulum in a side-to-side motion, and say, "This is my 'no.'" Do that a few times until it starts to feel natural for you. There. You've got your two assigned pendulum movements, your "yes" and your "no"!

What to Do If You Get "Switched"

If you try to use a pendulum when you're stressed, upset, or exhausted, you may find something strange happens. In that state, if you hold the pendulum over your palm, you may see that it's not making the movement you're used to seeing. Instead, it's swinging the way it normally does over the *back* of your hand. And if you hold it over the back of your hand, it makes the motion it usually does over your palm!

What's going on? You've gotten "switched." That means your energy is temporarily out of balance, and so you won't be able to get accurate "yes" or "no" answers or do any clearing.

However, there's no cause for alarm! Often you can bring yourself back into balance by just taking a nice deep breath and telling yourself to rebalance. If that doesn't work, drink some water, maybe have a snack, get a breath of fresh air, and then come back and try again. Perhaps move to a different chair, as you might have been sitting in an area of stress that made your system react like this.

After trying one or all of these solutions, is the pendulum making the usual movements again? If so, great. If not, you may need a good night's sleep; when you come back, the pendulum will work for you just fine. It's only a temporary situation, so don't worry about it. A big part of this work is trusting the process and not trying to force things.

How Using a Pendulum Affects Your Brainwaves

A pendulum is sometimes called a dowsing instrument. You may have never heard of dowsing; if you have, it may have been about someone dowsing to find underground water for a well. Dowsing is simply a way of getting information by tapping into your greater intuitive awareness without all the chatter in your head that usually blocks it, and a pendulum is just one tool that helps us do that. One of the remarkable things about a dowsing instrument, scientists have found, is that learning to use it has a measurable and amazingly positive effect on your brainwaves.

There are four different types of brainwaves: beta, alpha, theta, and delta. Beta is the one that's active when you're awake and in your everyday state of mind. Alpha is what you experience when you're feeling peaceful and content, and also during gentle meditation. Theta shows up when you're asleep and dreaming, and it also corresponds to the times you're so relaxed that creative ideas and instant solutions to problems suddenly emerge. Delta occurs during very deep, dreamless sleep, and it's also active during the very deepest meditative states.

Researchers studied the brainwaves of people while they were using a pendulum and found that during this process, there is an increase in alpha waves, the state you enter when you're peacefully happy. This was measurable even in people just beginning to learn how to use a pendulum. In terms of alpha waves, the dowsers' brains responded nearly identically to the brain of someone meditating. (So fascinating, considering how that meditation teacher in my workshop compared clearing to "accelerated meditation"!)

As people gained experience in dowsing, their theta waves began to increase (the very relaxed phase when creative ideas emerge). Over time, as they continued using the pendulum, their delta waves became active as well (the state of mind usually reached only during the deepest levels of meditation)!

But that's not all. The researchers found that as people became more practiced, they remained in heightened alpha and theta brainwave states even when they *weren't* dowsing. Most remarkably, highly experienced dowsers had *all four* brainwave states active *at the same time!* This was something that they hadn't seen in testing even the most accomplished Indian yogis.

What this means is that using a pendulum expands your consciousness, and this lasts even when you're not actively dowsing. Just the act of using a pendulum transforms your awareness.

You're Ready to Do a Clearing!

So now you know your personal "yes" and "no" movements. You know how to check to see if you're switched and what to do if you are. And you've learned how transformative it can be simply to use that pendulum. This means you're ready to move on to the next stage: doing a personal clearing!

chapter 4

How to Clear Personal Energy Fields

Simply by picking up that pendulum, you've already started developing your abilities. The next step is to use it to do a clearing for someone. You learn and gain confidence in clearing by actually *doing* it.

Rest assured, in all the years I've been teaching, there's never been anyone who couldn't learn how to clear, not even left-brained engineer husbands who were dragged to my course by their eager wives. In fact, it's sometimes the left-brained people who find it easiest to learn because it's devoid of what they consider magical thinking or mumbo jumbo!

If you were to watch me do a personal clearing for someone, it would just look like we were sitting having a chat, with one exception: I'd be swinging a pendulum. Clearing someone doesn't involve any physical touch (unless you count the fact that you often get a hug at the end!).

When you're first learning to clear, it's best to practice by clearing another person. Of course, you can clear yourself as well, but when you're first developing your skills, you won't be very effective. This is because you're too close to your own stuff; your own energy is so completely familiar to you that you won't find much to clear. Later on, once you've had more experience, you absolutely can clear yourself easily and effectively using the same technique here. But you need practice to get to that point, and you get that by clearing other people.

Ideally, you can work in person with a friend so you can talk to them as you clear them and so they can give you feedback. This is the quickest way to learn. However, if there's no one handy nearby, you can choose anyone you know, even if you can't meet in person. After all, energy isn't affected by distance or geography; I do clearings on the phone every day with people all over the world. Simply set up a time to talk on the phone or through a video chat such as Skype.

As a last choice, you can do a clearing without speaking to your friend in real time because just as distance doesn't matter, neither does timing. However, it's harder to learn this way because you don't have immediate feedback, so I don't encourage it. If you choose to proceed, then arrange to talk, text, or e-mail them soon after the clearing so you can discuss what happened while it's still fresh in your mind. They may also be able to validate any impressions you had or talk about any shifts they felt during the clearing.

If you're going to clear a friend who's at a distance from you, ask their permission first. You may know in your heart that they definitely need this help! However, especially in the early stages of your learning, your earnest desire can affect the clearing process. This can then create a situation where you're forcing the issue or having an attachment to a certain outcome. Getting permission from the other person will help lessen the chance of that happening.

Later on, we'll get into the what/how/why of the clearing process, but one of the main skills you'll first need to develop is not to race up into your head to try to figure out the mechanics of how to "do" a clearing! Instead, your job right now is to practice learning how to drop into a state that's more about *being* than about *doing* or analyzing. And that's what I'm about to guide you through.

The Five Steps before You Begin Any Clearing

These are the steps you will always take before you begin any clearing:

1. Check to see if you're switched.

Swing the pendulum over the palm of your hand to see if it's making the kind of movement it usually does there, whether that's spinning in a circle, side to side, or whatever motion you now know is yours. (You can also check it over the back of your hand too if you want to be doubly sure.)

If it makes its normal movement, that means your own energy is balanced enough; you're available to do a clearing. But if it doesn't, then it's likely you're switched and will be unable to clear. This usually happens only if you're stressed, tired, or upset. (Refer to the advice in Chapter 3 about how to get unswitched.)

This is the only time that you hold your free hand under the pendulum—to check whether you're switched. From this point on, you do not hold the pendulum over your hand. You simply hold it in a relaxed fashion, in midair.

2. Become aware of your feelings.

Take a nice deep breath and come into the moment. Relax and become aware of your feelings. How does your body feel? Do you notice any tension or discomfort somewhere? What is your emotional state?

What you're doing is taking a baseline reading of what's going on for *you*, before you tune in to someone else's energy. This makes it easier to notice any changes in how you feel during the clearing. Once you start clearing, any changes that you feel will most likely be your system sensing *their* energy. This will also help you recognize the subtle feelings you can have during a clearing that are actually signs of their releasing stress, old issues, or stuck energy.

3. Ask if it's appropriate to proceed.

Give your pendulum another little swing to start it moving and ask, "Is it appropriate to proceed?" Then wait a few moments to see if it makes your "yes" movement or your "no" movement.

If you get a "no": You must trust that. It could be that the person you want to clear isn't ready for it, the time isn't right, it might be too much for your ability at this point, or any number of reasons. It is essential to trust the answer that you get and not try to push the issue. You can check again after a few minutes, or the next day, or a week from now; it doesn't matter. What matters is that you don't try to force your will on the situation—you wouldn't be doing a clearing then anyhow. You'd be in the wrong state of mind, one that could actually detrimentally affect that person's energy or your own.

If you get a "yes": You can move forward to do the clearing!

4. Inform the other person.

Tell your friend to relax and just be aware of their feelings while you do the clearing. Let them know that they might have emotions come up, old memories could emerge, or they might sense something physically, and it can be helpful to discuss this either during or after the session.

5. Settle into a calm, open, wondering state of mind.

There's a certain state of mind to maintain while you do this work, one that can be described as "passive wondering." In other words, have a neutral and receptive attitude of *I wonder what will come up to be cleared* or *I wonder what I'll feel in this part of the clearing.* You are not looking for any particular issue, and you are not required to find or fix any specific problem. Your job is just to stay present and relaxed—just calmly open to whatever will come.

Clearing the First Field: Disturbing Effects of Others

Now you're ready to start. There are a total of six different energy fields that can be cleared in any session, and you always work with them in a specific order. Let's practice clearing the very first field, just to give you some experience of what this work is like, and then in the next chapter we'll continue on to the rest.

This first field is where you *always* start when you do a clearing for anyone. I've never found this vitally important field addressed in any other kind of energy work, yet it has a profound impact on your well-being on every level. It's named the Disturbing Effects of Others (DEO) field.

I always tell my clients, "This has less to do with you and more to do with how you've been affected by the people and places around you." In other words, the disturbing effects of others. It could be the stress surrounding you at the office that you carry home with you at the end of the day. It could be an old boyfriend who's still unwilling to let you go, sending his needy feelings your way like a little ribbon of energy that attaches to your field. It might be an imbalance that's been stuck in your energy for decades, like some of the tension in your childhood home when your parents fought, or a little of the frenzied atmosphere of the hospital emergency room you were in after an accident years ago.

When my son was in high school, and before he learned to drive, I'd drive him to and from school each day. The parking lot where I waited for him every afternoon was located at the other end of the athletic field, behind a thick grove of trees, so I couldn't actually see the building from where I sat. But I knew the moment the doors flew open and the students started to stream out because something akin to a wave from a nuclear blast slammed into my car! All those raging hormones, pent-up energy, and teenage angst blew across the land and specifically in the direction of the parking lot where the parents waited for their kids. Sitting in my car, I'd feel the wave hit and immediately my system reacted by going into clearing mode without my even having to try. Then a few minutes later, here would come the first few teens straggling along the path through the trees. That experience alone convinced me how important it is to clear DEOs!

All these vibrations can get velcroed to our energy fields over the years. As they accumulate, they weigh us down and continually stress our systems in invisible ways—and we wonder why we feel so worn out!

What Might Clear in the DEO Field

Often the first things that come up to be released in this field are how this person is currently being affected by the energy of the people they live with or work with. For example, when I clear someone who works in a large corporate setting, I often feel waves of tension that they've soaked in from all the people around them at work each day.

After the current stress in someone's DEO field lets go, it's common for older layers to emerge as the clearing continues. It's as if that first overlay has to go before the things that have been stuck underneath for years can be released. Sometimes I feel the energy of their mother or father as influences from their childhood clear. Or I may sense something toxic from long ago, such as the time I smelled the strong odor of cigarettes from a client who didn't smoke. But then he remembered that his roommate who had moved out five years before had been a chain smoker. The invisible residue of the smoke from the decade they lived together lingered in his energy field.

Every time you clear DEOs for someone, new layers can come up to clear; not everything clears in just one session.

How to Clear the First Field: Disturbing Effects of Others

Once you've done those five preliminary steps previously described, you can start the clearing! Here's what to do next:

1. Silently ask your pendulum, "Is there anything to clear in Disturbing Effects of Others?"

This is the one field where there is *always* something to clear, because you take things on here every day. During a trip to the grocery store, it's likely the bag boy isn't just packing the bananas into your shopping bag; he's probably also adding some of his personal frustration for you to carry home too! So your pendulum should always indicate a "yes" here.

If you get a "no": It's likely you have just gotten switched, or your mind has wandered and you're no longer present. It's also very possible that you're nervous about doing this right, and so you've tensed up too much. It's important to have a calm confidence that you can do this—even if you have to fake that feeling at first!

If you *do* get a "no" to this question, realize this is part of the learning process. All it might take to get back on track is to ease your anxiety by cracking a joke, or just taking a deep breath. You might take a break and come back to the clearing a few minutes later, or have someone clear *you* and then try again. But don't proceed if your pendulum says "no," because that's an indication you're temporarily unable to make enough of a connection to their energy.

If you get a "yes": You can begin to clear.

2. Holding your pendulum, tell yourself that you're now going to start clearing Disturbing Effects of Others.

3. Give the pendulum a swing to get it going.

At this point, you may notice that your pendulum soon starts to move in a brand-new way! Just like it swings in a certain manner to show you "yes" or "no," it may move in a different way to show you that clearing is happening. Its motion will change once again when the clearing is complete. Remember, it's basically a little biofeedback tool that lets you know when your system is experiencing something.

For example, when I use a pendulum, my "yes" is a vertical, up-and-down swing and my "no" is a horizontal, side-to-side swing. But when I'm clearing, my pendulum swings in a circle. When the clearing is complete, it changes its motion to an up-and-down "yes" movement so I know it's finished.

Rest assured, there's no one right way for your pendulum to move. It doesn't *have* to make a third motion for clearing. For some people, their pendulum will just make their "yes" motion during the clearing and change to "no" when they're done. Or vice versa, it'll make their "no" movement during the clearing and change to a "yes" once they're done. The nice thing is that you don't have to magically know when you've started or finished clearing; the change in how the pendulum moves will be that signal for you.

4. As you let the pendulum swing, hold the thought in mind that you're clearing Disturbing Effects of others.

"But What Do I _Do_?"

And now you'll be thinking, *I don't know what to do! I don't know how to clear. What do I do? Should I create an intention? Should I send love?*

Western culture has trained us all our lives to think we have to "do" something to fix things. We've been taught to believe the world works in a linear, cause-and-effect way, even though everything around us shows us that's not true. In nature, everything is interconnected in the most subtle and intricate ways. As humans, we're all swimming in a great sea of consciousness, with our thoughts, our feelings, and our energy intermingling with incredible complexity. It's when we try to *do* something to change an issue that we come from a very limited understanding, and this often causes more problems in the short or long run.

This work is not about doing; it's about being. In other words, your job is not to try to do anything to or for the other person. You don't have to figure out what's wrong and then how to change it. You don't have to try to infuse them with love or healing. Instead, your job is to relax, become present with them in this moment, and make yourself available to feel. When you do that, your own energy opens to theirs in a unique way, and that energetic connection actually allows stress and tension held in their system to relax and release. (We'll talk more about this in Part III.)

It can be a foreign experience for us to simply "be." Every neuron in our brains will be protesting, "C'mon! You've got to do something, say something, focus on something!" And this is where our wonderful pendulum steps up to help. Here's what you can "do": silently repeat to yourself, *I'm clearing Disturbing Effects of Others,* and watch the swinging pendulum. This is one of the benefits of using a pendulum—as a focusing tool, to help keep you present in the moment.

As I said, you actually learn how to clear by doing clearings, and in the process, you'll develop your ability to just "be"! Remember, you're only in the initial stages right now, so trust that I'm here to guide you, and that soon you'll feel comfortable and easy with this work.

Watch the pendulum swing, be present, silently hold the thought *I'm clearing Disturbing Effects of Others,* and tune in to how you're feeling. This is all you need to do in order for the clearing to proceed.

What Are You Feeling?

Stay aware of your feelings while the pendulum is swinging: Are there any minor changes in how you feel, even if they're barely noticeable? When energy moves, it's usually not a thunderbolt from the sky! Especially when you're first learning, it's something you'd probably never pay attention to, a little whisper of a hint of a shadow of a feeling inside. Later on, after you've gotten some practice, it'll be much easier to know when you're sensing some energy.

Frankly, most people learning how to clear feel absolutely nothing. Then they think, *Here I am, waving this silly dangly thing around and feeling zip, zero, nada. I knew I couldn't do this.* This is completely normal when you're in these initial stages, and you may not feel anything for the first several weeks of practice. In fact, "feeling" is not required; whether or not you feel *anything*, you will still do a successful clearing.

Still, there are a few reasons why it's beneficial to pay attention to what feelings may come up when you're doing a clearing. One is that this helps to open up your intuitive channels. A wonderful side effect of doing this work is that your intuitive abilities can really soar. This is because as you practice, your system is also learning a new way of being, operating on a different level from your everyday state of mind. Learning to drop into clearing mode allows you to access information from sources you'd normally not be open to.

A second reason to notice what you're feeling during a clearing is that the person you're clearing may be able to confirm that this feeling does in fact have to do with their experience. You share that you just felt a wave of sadness, and they say, "I was just thinking about my dog who died last month." Or you say, "Huh, my mouth keeps feeling very pinched and tense," and they say, "My husband tells me I purse my lips all the time. I think I hold my tension in my mouth." This can be a good confidence boost for you, knowing that what you're sensing probably does relate to the person you're clearing.

Another important reason it's helpful to tune in and feel things while you're clearing is that it's training you to notice in your own life when you're being affected by the energy from someone else! In the course of our everyday lives, we're sponges for the energy around us, but we often don't recognize when this is happening. You're sitting at your desk and suddenly feel frustrated. You assume it's because this project you're working on isn't progressing as quickly as you'd like. True, that might be part of it, but it could also be due to the fact that the person in the office next to yours has just had an angry phone call and is broadcasting his frustration through the wall into your space.

Learning to feel subtle things during a clearing trains you to notice, in your own life, when you've just been hit with some energy that's not yours. You'll begin to recognize this earlier and earlier until you'll know it the moment it happens. With that awareness alone, you are empowered to not take it on. You won't have to whip out your pendulum in the middle of a staff meeting!

Different Ways of Sensing When You Do a Clearing

Although you may feel nothing while you're still learning, after you get more practice, you may begin to notice feelings or impressions as you clear someone. We each have unique ways we sense things during a clearing.

Some people tend to feel waves of emotions move through their awareness. Others have mostly physical sensations, such as a twinge or a warmth somewhere in their bodies. You may see colors in your mind's eye, get images, or even hear words as you clear. A few people in workshops have found that song lyrics spontaneously came to mind that seemed to match the kinds of issues that were releasing!

One woman was discouraged at first because she wasn't getting any impressions. Then she suddenly realized that her sense of smell was her special talent. She was aware of different scents as she cleared but thought at first that it was just her imagination. We all soon became jealous of her ability to smell things like roses or chocolate cake with each field she cleared!

Remember to ask the friend you're clearing to also quietly stay aware of how they're feeling during the session; this will help them possibly notice things shifting, which can be encouraging for them. Sometimes they'll have similar sensations to those you're feeling, and that can be inspiring for both of you. But it's also not unusual for them to feel nothing at all; again, that doesn't impact the effectiveness of the clearing. Even if neither of you feels anything, the clearing is happening. Energy is invisible, subtle, and silent, and for most people, it takes training and practice to sense its movements. As you do more clearings, you'll gain more and more awareness in this way.

Before we talk about how to personally deal with the sensations you may have during a clearing, let's first discuss how you should share them with the person you are clearing. Then, in Chapter 6, we'll discuss when during a clearing you should share your feelings and how the actual process of that might go.

How to Share Your Intuitive Impressions

As you do this work and increase your ability to drop into an open, receptive state, your intuitive channels can really start to open up as well. But intuitive information usually isn't so kind as to give you a nice crisp, clear message! Instead, you may glimpse a fleeting image in your mind's eye or hear a few vague words, and it can be difficult to know what to make of that. As a result, you can get caught up in trying to analyze things, or expect your friend to know and explain to you what this means, which usually isn't possible.

The more you turn toward intuitive impressions and relax into them to welcome them, the more you'll develop your ability to get a better sense of the message coming through. Eventually these impressions will become like a trail of breadcrumbs you can follow to get to a deeper meaning.

So if you receive intuitive impressions during the clearing, don't get too caught up in trying to make sense of them. In most cases, the information is about something to do with the other person, not you. If you try to interpret what comes to mind, you're probably running it through the filter of your own personality and life experiences, so what comes out ends up being meaningless for your friend.

In other words, if you get an image of a rabbit, that might bring up pleasant memories of the Easter Bunny, or it might make you remember that you've been wanting to spend more time out in nature. On the other hand, the person you're clearing may have had a pet bunny as a child and what was releasing had to do with what was happening in their life at that time. The best action is to simply describe any feelings or impressions as raw information, without trying to make sense of it, because your interpretation might make it unrecognizable to them—just tell them you had an image of a rabbit!

It's best not to instruct your friend to figure out what your impressions mean either. For one thing, that puts them into their head to analyze things, which is not what we want. We want people to stay with their feelings even after the clearing because that allows their system to continue to process and relax into this new energy. Another reason is that you might be completely wrong about what you sensed! After all, no one is a clear channel. This is so essential to remember because some people too easily go into fear. If you tell your friend that you saw an airplane in your mind's eye and ask what they think it means, they may immediately decide that they should cancel their upcoming trip! You never want to leave someone with fearful feelings.

Be aware that many people will be looking for some "story" to explain things, and it can be tempting to give them one! One workshop student did a clearing where she got an image of teetering on the edge of a cliff and feeling frightened. The emotions associated with this vision were so strong, she felt sure this must be a memory of a past life for the person she was clearing. She ended up telling the woman that she'd been a princess in a past life hundreds of years ago and had thrown herself off a cliff because she was being forced to marry someone she didn't love! Yet if the student had just conveyed the image and feelings she got, it would have made sense to the woman she was clearing, who had been anguishing over a life-changing decision and had literally been saying to herself that she felt as though she were teetering on the edge of a cliff!

For all these reasons, when I work with someone, I tell them, "As I'm clearing, I sometimes feel sensations, or emotions, or get intuitive impressions. If I do, I'll share the information with you. But if this happens, each of us has a different job to do. My job is to share the raw data and not try to interpret what it might mean so that my own personal filter doesn't affect things. If you can't relate to it, your job is to not try to make it fit just because I said it!

"What I sense could just be how my own system is experiencing something releasing in your energy field, or I could have misunderstood an impression due to its vagueness. Or it could be predictive, and something may happen two weeks in the future that completely relates to what I described during the clearing."

It's a wonderful side benefit of clearing that intuitive information can come through, but what's most important is that clearing is happening! There will be many powerful releases in their energy, so remember that and don't try to turn this into a psychic reading.

How to Deal with What You Feel Physically

Most of the time, if you do sense something physically as you're clearing someone, it'll be small and fleeting. For example, you may feel a tingle somewhere in your body, or you just feel "different" for a few seconds. Or it may be a more obvious and distinct physical sensation. Whether the feeling is barely discernible or quite pronounced, this is basically just information. In other words, it's how your system is noticing the energy that's coming up to be cleared. That tingle is just a sensation in response to what's clearing; it's not that there's anything wrong with your body.

One way to help us understand this is to compare it to all the other ways we get "information" in everyday life with our regular five senses. For instance, let's say you go to visit a friend, and when you walk in her front door, you smell curry. So you know she probably just cooked a curry dinner. You don't freak out and run away, thinking a problem in her house has made something go terribly wrong with your nose! It's just that one of your senses has let you know about some information in that environment.

When you have a physical sensation during a clearing, it's just information that your system has noticed. Once you leave your friend's house, you won't be smelling curry any longer, and once you finish a clearing, you won't still be feeling tingly! It wasn't "yours"; it was something releasing from the other person's energy field, and this was how you experienced it.

There are two main reasons you may feel something physically during a clearing: One is that it's how your body is reacting to the energy as it clears. The second is that there's some stress that's been locked into that part of the other person's body, and you're feeling it shift and release. So if, for instance, you felt a little contraction in your throat as you cleared your friend, you have a few options about what to say:

1. Simply describe the sensation you had, and make sure to add that this could just be how your system was experiencing what was clearing and it might have had nothing to do with *their* throat at all.

2. Explain that a difficult emotion or memory can get stuck in ways that affect certain parts of the body that have nothing to do with illness. For instance, a contracting sensation in the throat might actually be related to a struggle with feeling like they can't speak up. If you find that your friend relates to that, it can make the clearing

even more meaningful for you both and open up a deeper conversation.

3. Decide not to mention what you felt in your throat. Just because you felt something, it doesn't mean you are required to share it with your friend. If they're the kind of person who's anxious or tends to make mountains out of molehills, it may not be helpful to give them an opportunity for something new to worry about!

If you decide to describe a sensation in a clearing to another person, be very aware that it's easy for them to begin to worry they have some disease and you are feeling its "symptoms." If they can't relate to the sensation you describe, assure them this is just how your system is experiencing the clearing so they don't go into unnecessary fear.

How to Understand Emotions You May Feel

It's not unusual to feel some emotions pass through your awareness as you're doing a clearing. For instance, a wave of sadness or frustration may come up, or you may suddenly feel lonely. These feelings are likely associated with what's releasing for your friend. It's essential to recognize them as just signs of energy moving, as some information you've tuned in to during the clearing process.

It can be both fascinating and deeply moving to have the experience of actually sensing another person's feelings: in other words, true empathy. But there's a distinction between feeling an emotion and getting lost in it. If you tune in to your friend's sadness about their divorce, it can be too easy to get caught up in feeling so sorry for them—or to remember your own divorce and then get personally flooded with emotion. If either of those things happens, it's like falling out of the boat into the water. You become so awash in the feeling that you start to drown in it, and then you're no longer in balance and available to clear.

Imagine a doctor treating a patient in crisis: They don't get caught up in their patient's panic or stressed by their own painful memory about a time they suffered. They maintain a calm attitude, being compassionately present but not letting their own emotions run away with them. If they didn't, they wouldn't be able to make good decisions about the treatment.

Another example that might help is to imagine the scenario of a parent and child. Suppose you've taken your child to play in the park, and the child falls down or has a fright. They come running to you, shrieking and crying, and what do you do? Do you also freak out and scream and cry as well? Of course not! It's not that you don't care; in fact, your heart goes out to them, and you want to make them feel better. But you know that in order to do that, you can't get upset; and you know there's actually nothing to be upset about. So you scoop them up and embrace them with a calm, loving energy, and that's what allows them to let go of that terrified state and come back into balance.

When you're doing a clearing, you don't have a detached attitude. You feel genuine empathy and compassion for the other person, but you maintain "nonattachment": you don't get swept up in their drama or let it trigger your own. You hold a caring presence and stay mindful that the clearing is bringing healing to the situation. I love the way Russell Targ and Jane Katra describe this kind of "presence" in their book *Miracles of Mind*:

The practice of quieting one's mental noise and creating coherence with a patient allows a healer's caring intentions and state of consciousness to become an avenue of this spiritual healing. . . . A healer's prayerful state makes available a type of "healing template," which appears to activate a patient's own self-healing capabilities. . . . It is actually an information transaction, involving a relationship in which need, helping intentions, and quiet minds are the important elements. . . .

The basis of this spiritual healing resides in an attitude of openness and attunement to a greater universal mind, working through a person with helping intentions, in an environment of trust and surrender of personal ego.

There's an even greater and more profound benefit that comes from paying attention to what you feel when you clear someone. It not only develops your ability to bring balance and flow to another person's life but also simultaneously trains your system to respond to your own life in a completely new way, to let go of your stress the moment it appears. You're learning how to relate to all your experiences without going into reaction in your usual ways. With each clearing that you do, you create a more spacious and peaceful place for you to stand within your own life. (We'll talk more about this in Part III.)

A Note for Highly Sensitive People

If you identify as highly sensitive, you might worry that it could be too intense an experience for you to open up and connect with another person's energy. You're already feeling too much, for heaven's sake, and the last thing you want is to feel *more* and be put into overwhelm!

In fact, this work doesn't expose your system to anything new at all. What you're actually doing is something you've already been experiencing 24/7 for your entire life. Whether you've been aware of it or not, you've always been open to the energy of other people, but without the ability to turn it off. Now, with clearing, you'll still be open but you'll be doing it with *conscious control.*

The truth is that learning to clear is like being given the solution to finally managing your sensitivity and not being so inundated by the information around you. You now have a way to clear anything that you've taken on, and through learning to do this work, you're developing the ability to become immediately aware when something you're feeling is "not yours." Just having that mindful moment can keep you from being impacted by it.

There's one more amazing gift that this work brings to sensitive people. What I've found is that learning to use the pendulum to do clearings gives you an "on/off" button. In other words, your system gets trained so that when you pick up your pendulum, you're "on" open for business, available to the energy around you. When you put down your pendulum, that's the signal to your system that you're "off"—closed for business and with reestablished boundaries. You have gained conscious control of your energy system—and this may well be the very first time in your life that you have the experience of actually turning *off* your sensitivity!

Within just a few weeks of developing this new skill, what you've learned can start to click into place in your everyday life. You don't have to walk around holding a pendulum all day. Just through the practice of clearing, you gain an automatic ability to open and close to the world around you as needed. With time, you can even refine that control so that you're not just open or closed but instead can choose to open up 20 percent to the information around you, or 85 percent, or whatever is appropriate to the situation.

Learning clearing teaches your system how to develop healthy energetic boundaries and how to feel safe again, to walk through the world without being overwhelmed by everything that you feel. I've had so many highly sensitive people tell me over the years that this work has changed their lives—and I can certainly relate.

If You Don't Think of Yourself as Sensitive

Of course, you don't have to be a highly sensitive person to be affected by other people's energy! It happens to all of us every day. (Remember what we discussed in Chapter 1 about how we're all affected by the invisible energy around us?) If you're in a staff meeting and you start feeling depressed, well, it may be your depression or it may be that the person sitting next to you is broadcasting their depressed feeling. Here you are, minding your own business, and suddenly your mood plummets.

In normal life, we usually don't realize when an emotion has infiltrated from somewhere else. If we start to feel depressed, of course we identify that feeling as ours. Then as our mind and body believe it, we *can* become depressed. *Oh, what's the use, life is hard, nothing ever works out . . .* If you're around depressed people every day, it's possible to take those feelings as yours and sink deeper and deeper into them.

As you learn to do this work and start to sense subtle things happening during a clearing, you're training your system to recognize when a feeling belongs to someone else and to then respond to it in a new way. Very soon, if you get slammed with a depressed feeling, you might immediately say to yourself, "Whoa, that's not mine!" Often, that awareness is enough to keep you from absorbing it; you don't have to quickly pull out your pendulum and clear! Then that feeling goes wandering off to look for someone who *will* believe it's theirs.

How Long It Takes to Clear Each Field

Usually, it takes only a few minutes to clear any of the fields. But when you're first learning, it's not unusual for one of two things to happen: clearing a field can take just a few moments *or* it can seem to take forever!

If you clear one of the fields in about five seconds, it's not that you're the world's best energy worker or that the person is highly enlightened and has little that needs to be released! More likely, your lack of confidence interfered with your ability to relax and be present. It's normal to have some performance anxiety in the early stages of learning anything. Alternatively, you could have been trying so hard to "help," to make things better, you were no longer in clearing mode and were unable to maintain a calm and neutral state of mind. When these kinds of situations happen, your pendulum can change its swing to indicate you're finished soon after you've started, or even just cease moving at all. This reflects that you've stopped being able to clear, not that there is nothing left to clear.

Or the opposite might happen—your pendulum could keep swinging and swinging and not change its motion, so that 15 minutes later, the clearing in this field seems to be still going on! This could be an indication that you were doubting yourself, or trying too hard, or tightly concentrating on technique. In cases like these, you're not actually still clearing; you're back up in your head, and your pendulum is spinning just like your thoughts.

It's common in the early stages to have things like this happen. No worries—it's not a problem. As is the case with any skill, there's a learning curve here. So if clearing DEOs finishes in a flash or seems to go on forever, just take a relaxing breath and begin again. With a little more experience, these things won't happen any longer. It'll take a few minutes to clear the field, and your pendulum will accurately indicate when you're done.

There are a total of six energy fields, which we clear one at a time during this process. This is part of what makes clearing so powerful; its gentle and subtle approach circumvents any resistance in the other person's system and prevents you from trying to work with too much at any one time. You've learned how to clear the first energy field, so let's move on now to clear the other five fields!

chapter 5

Continuing with the Personal Clearing

the inner fields

The second through sixth fields are known as the inner fields; they are the ones that have to do with your own personal stress and imbalance. This takes us to the heart of this work.

Much of clearing is based on the ancient principles of Chinese medicine, including what is called the Five Element Cycle, which is said to be like a map of the energy system of any living being. If you've read books about feng shui, face reading, or Chinese medicine, you probably encountered this concept before. The elements are named Water, Wood, Fire, Earth, and Metal. However, it's not that the Chinese believed the world was literally made of these substances. Instead, they are simply descriptive terms for the different qualities of energy that make up your system.

Each of the inner fields corresponds to one of the elements. With each, there are many different types of stuck or stressed energy that can release or rebalance. But there are certain patterns of issues that can consistently come up to be cleared in each field. Knowing these patterns can help you recognize possible meanings in the impressions you may get as you clear. But it's not at all necessary to know anything about the elements in order to do energy clearing because this book gives you a description of the most frequent issues each field includes in terms of this work. So you're not at any disadvantage if these are new concepts to you; in fact, you may well be better off because you won't have to unlearn any misconceptions!

❦

Second Field: Water
(Fear, Trust, Ancestors, Inherited Issues)

The second energy field you will clear has to do with what's called the Water Element. In the Water field, the following are common themes that the clearing may deal with.

Fear

Clearing the Water field often releases any issues where fear is blocking you. This isn't simple anxiety or worry; it's the kind of deep, cold, primal dread that can be a paralyzing force in life, causing your energy to freeze and keep you from moving forward because no matter what direction you consider, there's something to be afraid of.

This fear can be below the level of your awareness but can imperceptibly affect your feelings, your choices, and your perceptions. Even when you're conscious of fear blocking your progress in life, you often don't recognize how pervasive it is under the surface, like underground streams running beneath the earth.

Trust

Sometimes the imbalances in this field aren't ones you'd immediately identify as "fear"; instead, they show up as a tendency to be insecure or have a constant sense of being all alone in the world. They can also be associated with feeling like an outsider, or a belief that others are leaving you out in important ways, or at the extreme, abandonment issues. These problems all still revolve around fear, which actually comes from a lack of trust—in your own natural courage, strength, and wisdom; in whether the people you need will really be there for you; and even in life to care for and protect you. You might carry a certain degree of these kinds of issues at times, but in some cases, they could flood into all aspects of your beliefs and behavior. If the world is a scary place, how could you ever feel secure about venturing out to fulfill your life journey?

You can be born with an innate supply of fear and lack of trust as part of the patterns of your personality, or you can also develop it through life experiences that leave you convinced that you'll always be alone, no matter what you try. Either way, these feelings can make you tread water in life rather than trust that you can swim with the current and enjoy the wonderful adventure you were designed to have.

Every time you clear this second field for someone, it releases layers of their fear and allows them to relax a little bit more into a sense of trust that Life loves them, that others want them to succeed, and that they have the strength to deal with whatever comes their way.

As fear starts to clear, what emerges is faith in your own deep inner power and your intuitive wisdom to know how to navigate life on your own. You start to feel more secure in the place you stand right now, instead of believing you're all alone and in peril. Clearing this field allows you to move forward with a sense of ease and flow.

Ancestors

Another kind of issue that can come up for clearing in this field has to do with the concept of what the Chinese call "Ancestors." There are two sides to its meaning, one beneficial and one detrimental.

In Chinese culture, when a family member dies and passes over, they're believed to transform into an "Ancestor" who beams blessings from the other side to their living relatives. All the wisdom and power they accumulated in their life is now available to be transmitted to their descendants, to bless and benefit them for the rest of their lives on earth. This is actually the purpose for which feng shui was first developed thousands of years ago: to select the sites of graves. Where do we bury Grandfather so his blessings will be beamed toward our house and not the neighbor's by mistake?

In most of Asia to this day, their sense of connection to their ancestors is much more a part of the culture than it is in the West. We Westerners operate on the assumption that it's all up to us to make our way in life. We have to figure it out ourselves and work hard to make things happen, to reach our goals so we can be successful. We're told to "lean in," to put forth effort or we'll never achieve anything. But to the Chinese, it's ridiculous to think that we're somehow disconnected from our source, our ancestors, and are all alone in the world. They believe that the essence, power, and wisdom of our ancestors support our journey, if we would just open to that rich resource.

In the body, Ancestor energy is said to be stored in the kidneys. You have two kidneys, one on each side of your back. You can visualize them like the two hands of your Ancestors being held up to support you, and download their deep power to help you on your way. Rather than "lean in," we're actually meant to lean *back* on those hands, with the trust that it's not all up to us to figure everything out. Rather than exhaust ourselves in the hamster wheel of work-work-work, we become one with the flow. We receive intuitive guidance and effortlessly move forward in the right direction.

Clearing this field can help us recover our connection to our essence, which is the inherited power of the generations who came before and a deep source of life-energy. We relax and are carried along like a leaf riding the current in the river.

Your connection with your ancestors has a powerfully beneficial impact on your life. But if you're one of the many people who came from a dysfunctional family, you may feel an aversion to the thought of an energetic connection with your ancestors. It can help to consider that no one carries their earthly dramas or toxic personalities with them to the other side! However, an option you can try is to imagine the ancestors as not part of your actual family line but instead wise sages on the other side who

65

are available to help you in the same way, with strength and wisdom accumulated over the ages.

Inherited Issues

There can also be a detrimental effect from your lineage. Inherited issues are energetic imbalances that are passed down through the family line. In other words, if one of your ancestors had a traumatic experience that changed them and caused a problem in their life, that imbalance could be transmitted in the family DNA to each subsequent generation until it lands in your life to create a problem for you as well. No matter how much personal work you do to try to heal the issue, it won't succeed because the issue didn't originate with you—it's not yours to heal.

Even Western science is now discovering this aspect of inherited issues. Through the new field of epigenetics, we've learned that things that happened to our ancestors can change their DNA, which can then be passed down through the family line to future generations. Researchers have found lasting epigenetic effects in the physical health as well as the emotional nature of descendants. A traumatic experience for Great-Great-Grandfather Henry in World War I could have created an energetic imbalance that you might inherit, but it might not be apparent that it began long ago in the family history. Instead, it might show up in your life in ways that make it look like a personal problem of your own or a pattern of problems shared by family members, each of whom is struggling with it in their own way.

When you clear the Water field, it can address the release of detrimental inherited issues and/or connect you to the beneficial support of your ancestors. However, do not ask to specifically clear inherited issues or reconnect to ancestors' power. Just hold the thought in mind that you're clearing "Water"; then, if there is anything that can be released or rebalanced at this time, it will do so. When an inherited issue is cleared, or when a connection to the blessings and support of your ancestors is reestablished, it can have a transformative effect on your life, freeing up what had previously been trapped positive life force!

Clearing the Water Field

To clear this field, you simply continue on to it after clearing the first field, DEO. First, check whether you're switched by briefly holding the pendulum over your palm, just to make sure it makes the expected movement. If all is well, then take your palm away and hold the pendulum as usual.

Silently ask, *Is there anything to clear in Water?* If it says "yes," then proceed to clear.

Tell yourself, *I'm clearing the Water field*, and your pendulum will go into its clearing movement.

Stay present and be aware of what you're feeling. When this part of the clearing is complete, your pendulum will change its movement.

At this point, you can share any feelings or impressions you had with your friend, or you can wait until the entire clearing is complete to talk about it. When you do discuss it, let them know that they can talk to you about anything they felt or that came to their mind.

If you got a "no," that there isn't anything to clear for Water, trust that. It doesn't mean there's nothing here to clear, just that the time isn't right, you're not able right now, or the person isn't ready to release anything here yet. So if you get a "no," don't do any clearing for this second field; just go on to the third field.

❧

Third Field: Wood
(Anger, Forgiveness, Vision)

The third field has to do with the energy of what's called the Wood Element. In the Wood field, the following are some common themes in the energies that can need rebalancing.

Anger

What often comes up for clearing in this field are any issues where your feelings of anger are interfering with your life. We usually think of anger as a bad emotion because we mostly see it expressed in destructive ways. But Chinese medicine teaches that there can also be healthy, positive anger. If we trace this feeling back to its heart, it's actually a strong desire for change, a need to stop what's wrong, to create a new future. Healthy anger is what stimulates your drive, your ability to set a goal and achieve it. It's desire, like a booster rocket, that gets you moving into self-actualization.

But due to difficult life experiences, your healthy anger can get suppressed or be expressed with disharmony. The result is that despite your best efforts, you're not making the progress you want. This can be due to an old, old hurt that has lingered inside for so many years that it's no longer recognized for what it is. Or it might be because you are dealing with a current frustration in moving forward, one that keeps you locked into angry reaction far too often. Whatever the cause, when the energy of anger is out of balance, your sense of feeling in charge of your life is diminished.

If feelings of anger get stuck in your system, you can be caught in negativity or easily irritated or upset but not recognize the cause of this pattern. It can affect your sense of vitality that helps push you on toward your goals. If this continues over time, your vibrant outward drive, which is supposed to focus you forward in life, can instead gradually turn around to aim inward, with angry thoughts toward yourself. In other words, it creates depression, which Western psychology often defines as "anger turned inward." And if the depression continues, eventually what develops is total apathy, which is a complete absence of any drive, whether positive or negative.

Clearing this field can often result in reclaiming your hope and optimism, and the clarity and confidence to take action to achieve your goals. When this field is in balance, you feel more in control of your destiny, and you can become a benevolent force in the world to help create positive change and growth for us all.

Forgiveness

If someone has been hurtful to you in the past, it can be difficult to get over, no matter how many years have gone by. There can even be a sense of shame that this happened to you, as well as anger at yourself, as if you were at fault for letting it happen. This is part of what can cause anger to become stuck in your energy field for years into the future, and this blocks you from moving into the next stage of the process: the emergence of forgiveness.

When this third field is cleared, there can be a soft-ening into forgiveness, a letting-go of blame for yourself and for the person who harmed you. The result is that the hurt from this old mistreatment no longer affects how you choose to live. This can happen naturally and invisibly during the clearing.

It can also help to remember that no one behaves unkindly unless they are emotionally damaged. As the saying goes, "Hurt people hurt people." In other words, someone who was healthy in their heart of hearts never would have treated you that way. But because they were basically emotionally disabled, their behavior was hurtful.

If someone is physically disabled, it's usually appar-ent; for example, you can see that they're in a wheelchair. And if someone's in a wheelchair, you don't expect them to be able to climb the stairs with you. You may have to wait for them to find a ramp or an elevator or make spe-cial accommodations for them, but you don't get upset. You understand that their behavior is due to their physical challenges.

On the other hand, when someone is emotionally chal-lenged, it's often not so obvious. They look like a whole, functioning human being, so when they behave in an unhealthy way toward you, you take it personally and feel hurt. But what if you could reframe your view? They aren't able to behave in a healthy way because they're emotion-ally disabled. Visualize the person's emotional handicap as a physical one; picture them as physically challenged or ill in some way, and this can really help you move toward a place of soft forgiveness.

This forgiveness can extend to yourself as well. It's likely there was no way you could have known that the person was going to be so unkind to you. You had unreal-istic expectations of them because their disability wasn't visible. But now you've gained important knowledge that empowers you to protect yourself better in the future.

When Jessica came to me for a clearing, she was trying to recover from a difficult divorce. Her husband had been abusive, and he was still trying to harm her in every way he could during the divorce process. She was in such pain, not only from the abuse but also from blaming herself for being so loyal and giving him so much power over her. As I cleared this field for her, she suddenly got a vivid picture of looking down at her husband as a tiny little man barely as tall as her waist. Jessica said it was this image of an "emotional pipsqueak" that made her recognize who he really was, and she finally felt able to take back her power.

Vision

The Wood field also has to do with how easily you can create a vision of what you really want in life, and how well you can summon the insight to then form a realistic action plan to reach that destination.

Some people's personalities come packaged with a naturally low level of self-confidence that interferes with their believing in their vision and ability to accomplish it. Others started out inherently confident but were disempowered by someone early in life and so lost that sense of self-assurance. Either way, this kind of uncertainty can narrow the possibilities they can envision. They may struggle with believing they can even dare to dream or lack the clarity to form more than just vague ideas of where they might go with their life.

Additionally, if you're stuck in a hamster wheel of constant work, it limits your ability to envision a different future or how you might achieve it. Or if you tend to put everyone else's needs before your own, it prevents you from focusing on what *you* want. You may even feel guilty, as if it were selfish to think about your own needs.

An image in nature for healthy Wood Element energy is that of a plant breaking through the ground in the spring. Although it's just a tiny sprout, it can even crack solid concrete in its drive toward the sun. There's a plan programmed deep in its being that activates this strong "push" forward. We all have a plan like this, and clearing can release whatever is blocking us from accessing that plan, so that we regain our sense of direction in life.

Clearing the Wood Field

Just as you did when you cleared the first two fields, briefly check the pendulum over your palm to make sure you're still in balance. Then ask if there's anything to clear in the Wood field.

If you get a "yes," then go ahead and clear. If you get a "no," skip this field and move on to the fourth. There's not always something available to clear in each of these inner fields every time.

❀

Fourth Field: Fire
(Love, Joy, Healing the Heart)

The next field to clear is associated with what's called the Fire Element. The following are common themes in what often comes up to clear in Fire.

Love

What is sometimes addressed in the Fire field is how safe your heart feels to accept and to express love. This doesn't encompass only romantic love but also includes how you are in any friendship or relationship with another. Do you feel safe to allow someone fully into your heart? And are you able to show your own love for them in a healthy and positive way?

You may carry a belief that you have to lose weight or somehow make yourself better before someone can find you lovable. Or you may carry painful memories from past relationships that keep you locked into fear of rejection or of experiencing similar heartbreak again. If someone betrayed you in the past, you may struggle with being able to trust ever again.

Any obstacles to your own love for yourself can be mirrored in your blocks to loving others as well. Just as you may be too hard on yourself, you could also get stuck in judging people, rejecting them before they reject you, or being too rigid in what you require of a person before you can show them love.

This part of the clearing addresses any places in your energy that create obstacles to love. As the clearing happens, these areas may relax and release, opening new ways for you to experience love in your life. Sometimes when clearing this field for someone, you may even feel a stretching sensation in your own chest, as if your heart is expanding and opening more and more. This can be a reflection of what's happening for your friend's heart as you clear them, but it can also be a sign that your own heart is expanding its range. Clearing this field also broadens the ability of your heart to open to any heart you encounter and still feel safe.

Chinese medicine teaches that a healthy heart naturally protects itself; it can open or close as needed. Your heart is said to have a "Guardian of the Gate," whose job is to be discerning about who you let in, the pace at which they may enter, and just how far they're allowed to proceed. If the Guardian's doing their job, then you'll have a psychic sense about another person, intuitively knowing how quickly or slowly to develop the relationship and how much to trust them with your heart.

If your longing for love is an overriding force in your life, it can weaken the Guardian's discernment, and then the gate will swing open too easily. That's when you might get involved with someone who isn't worthy of your trust and so have your heart broken. If you've been hurt in the past, that can cause the Guardian to slam the gate shut and lock it tight to not let anyone in again.

It may not all happen in a single clearing, but it may be that after only a few clearings the Guardian regains their healthy discernment, and your heart feels able to be vulnerable, yet still safe, while experiencing love more fully than ever before.

Joy

This energy field is associated with the heart in other ways as well. In Chinese medicine, the emotion that relates to the heart is actually not love—it's joy. When the Fire field is clear, your heart is lit up with the joy of just being alive and the thrill of involving yourself fully in everything you do with passion and exuberance. You walk down the street beaming, feeling at one with each person who passes by.

You experience life this way when you're a small child, but soon your light may begin to dim due to painful experiences that make you feel unloved. At the same time, you're surrounded by adults whose light has already gone out, so you have few models for keeping the joy alive! So many people show a "lack of Fire": no light in their eyes, no radiance in their faces, no joy in their hearts. If you look through a series of your childhood photos, you may see your bright spirit in each for the first several years of your life, and then suddenly the rest of the photos in the second part of your childhood show that the light, your inherent joy, has dimmed or even disappeared.

But then again, things could also go to the opposite extreme. Instead of experiencing a lack of joy, that natural sense of excitement can amplify until it transforms into anxiety or erratic emotions. Healthy joy carries a sense of calm warmth; it's not out-of-control excitement. In Chinese medicine, your heart is said to go out during the day to exchange sparks of joy with other hearts. At night, it's meant to come home to your body and settle, calming itself into a state of peace so you can get a restful sleep. If the energy here is out of balance, you might experience insomnia at night. Or it might be that during the day you struggle with anxiety or feelings of emotional instability. If things get extremely out of balance in this field, the result can even be hysterical behavior, panic attacks, or post-traumatic stress disorder (PTSD).

Clearing in this field can restore peace to your heart and help you reclaim your joyful spirit so you're then able to discover and manifest your true passion in life.

Healing the Heart

We all experience some degree of heartbreak or even betrayal in life, and we do our best to recover and heal. But when your heart has been hurt, this can subtly influence your thoughts, feelings, and choices for years to come. It can make you reticent and afraid of being vulnerable again, or you may have difficulty allowing true intimacy. You may protect yourself by holding on to weight, keeping relationships superficial, or looking for an excuse to leave if you sense even the possibility of being hurt again.

You may not even recognize how your heart is still looking at the world through that filter of old pain or fear, and thus not see all the ways it's limiting you in life. In a clearing, you may feel a tightness at first as you tune in to how the person's heart feels, and then you may get a beautiful sense of gradual blossoming as their heart starts the journey back to wholeness.

There are other ways your heart can be in need of healing. In Chinese medicine, the heart provides a kind of psychic ability, an expansive consciousness that makes you aware of how others are thinking and feeling. It's with your heart that you sense when your friend is thinking of you or that your child needs you. It can be fun when, for example, you know who's just texted you before you even look at your phone! But there can be a downside to this ability as well.

If your Fire energy is out of balance, your psychic boundaries can become weakened. In other words, you become a kind of psychic sponge. You may be bombarded by the thoughts and feelings of the people around you, and this can put you in a state of emotional overwhelm where you feel too easily upset or scattered without knowing why. In this case, healing the heart means creating healthier psychic boundaries; you can still be open, but without taking on feelings that aren't even yours!

Lastly, your heart is considered to be the shock absorber for your experiences in the world. It's what helps you deal with daily upsets as well as more traumatic events. Your heart also transmutes this same kind of stress in all the frenzy of modern life. The noise, the crowds, and especially all the ways your attention is constantly on all your devices can affect your Fire energy. Being on your computer, tablet, or phone all day, and possibly even sleeping with your phone nearby all night, exposes you to constant stimulation that your heart energy has to contend with. Clearing this field can bring a growing ability to cope, as well as more discernment about your exposure to this kind of stress.

Clearing the Fire Field

Again, briefly hold the pendulum over your palm, just to check to make sure you're still in balance. If so, then you can proceed to see if there's anything that can be released here.

Ask your pendulum if there's anything to clear in the Fire field. If you get a "yes," then proceed. If you get a "no," just skip this field and move on to the fifth.

Fifth Field: Earth
(Safety, Support, Relationships)

The next stage of the clearing is for the Earth Element. As with each field, there are many different types of energy that can be released or rebalanced here. But there are certain issues that can consistently come up to be cleared with each of the Elements, and the following are some that are often addressed in the Earth field.

Safety

Clearing in this field can revolve around how rooted and safe you feel, how at home you are in your own life. In order to really believe you're safe, you need to have a sense of solid ground beneath your feet.

One way this is achieved is when you're in a place of satisfaction and contentment in your career. But if your career no longer seems like a fit, then you may lack that grounded feeling. Either you stay in the job and risk the repercussions of continued unhappiness, or you have to gamble on a new career and risk shaking the entire foundation of your life and your financial stability.

You'll also have a general sense of safety if you like where you live and have friends and family who accept you for who you are. However, if you're not satisfied with where you're living, then your energy won't feel settled, and you'll always want to pull up your roots and move. If there aren't enough people in your life who let you be you, then there's also no feeling of refuge, of belonging and acceptance. You need a sense of safety in every aspect of your life, but at any one time, there are likely areas where you don't quite feel it.

Sometimes imbalances in this field can be traced back to childhood, especially if there was little sense of safety at home. Emotionally volatile family members can leave your system still unsettled in adult life. In Chinese medicine, this field is also associated with the theme of "Mother," and in many ways, your mother is the one who's meant to provide you with a feeling of being protected and secure. But if you experienced a lack of nurturing from her, whether due to her emotional problems or circumstances beyond her control, that can also contribute to a deficit in feeling safe. For instance, if your mother had to work two jobs, she may not have been able to be there for you despite her best efforts. Any number of individual experiences could have caused you to feel unsafe when you were a child, and each of them contributes to this being a lifelong issue.

You might see a lack of feeling safe as the root cause of someone's struggle with their weight, or forming part of the reason why they accumulate clutter in their home. However, it may be a more subtle influence in the background, something that blocks their ability to put their thoughts into action or form lasting bonds. Clearing in this field often opens new ways for you to feel truly at home in the world and satisfied with your life.

Support

The need for support goes hand in hand with the need for a sense of safety, of course. The dictionary definition of "support" describes it as something that holds up, serves as a foundation. It withstands without giving way, with patience and tolerance. It is about sustaining a person, the mind, spirits, courage, etc., during trial or affliction.

Do you have enough true-blue people in your life who uphold you, sustain you, and believe in you? Who will always be there, no matter what, like the ground beneath your feet? If not, there can be a variety of ways that this imbalance shows up in your life.

A lack of support can equate to lack of resources and a corresponding difficulty fulfilling your dreams. For instance, you may find yourself living in a place where there aren't enough like-minded souls, or you may be caught in a career or family situation where you feel the people around you are unsupportive. You may keep trying to get your ideas off the ground but can never quite make the launch.

Another imbalance in this pattern can be your own lack of receptivity. If you're unable to take in nourishing support, you may exhaust yourself trying to do everything all by yourself. If you're unable to make use of the resources available to you, it'll be hard to bring your dreams to fruition.

Difficulty receiving is something that many people struggle with, and the issue may date to childhood when their mother wasn't able to be the nurturing presence they needed. This may not have been their mother's fault. For instance, if she had to spread her attention around a large family, or if she had to work while raising her children on her own, she wouldn't have had much left to give.

Whether there were circumstances out of your mother's control or her temperament wasn't a nurturing one, the end result can ripple into your adult life as a weakness in receptivity. If you weren't well nurtured in childhood, that means you didn't have much experience receiving. You didn't learn how, and so your receptivity muscles didn't get fully developed. Once you understand the source of the issue, you can become more able to recognize how and when it affects your experience in adult life.

No matter the cause or consequence of an issue with support, clearing in this field can transform your ability to take in nourishment. It could be in the literal sense, and your relationship with food could be revolutionized. You may also begin to notice people showing up for you in ways they hadn't before, offering to help or making connections for you. You may suddenly realize that you've lost your hesitation about asking for support, and you're now just naturally reaching out to others without feeling shy about it. And you may also start tending to your dreams more successfully, regaining the ability to be the gardener of your own soul.

Relationships

Relationships are such a vital part of life, whether they're romantic or with family and friends. They're your external source of safety and support; they allow you the opportunity to give and receive. They feed your spirit. When this field is in balance, you're able to form healthy bonds and maintain lifelong friendships. You feel genuinely cared for and fulfilled by your own sincere care for the people in your life. You have a sense of being protected without feeling smothered, of being embraced without being held back.

When there are stresses in relationships, whether current or lingering from the past, they can come up to be cleared in this field. Clearing can also bring new balance to how you manage your relationships. For example, you may struggle with boundaries with others and feel guilty about tending to your own needs. You may overgive, let people take advantage of you, or have trouble saying "no." You may spend too much of your energy worrying about others, and so tire yourself out simply because you're always flooding your thoughts out in their direction. This can cause you to lose your own strong center and affect how well you can fulfill your purpose in the world.

On the other hand, instead of being overly connected to people, you might feel isolated and lonely without *enough* of a sense of connection to community, to people who are or feel like family to you. Trudging through life alone, carrying the weight of having to do everything on your own, can be wearying for your body and your soul. You might feel this way even if you're married or have lots of friends and family in your life. As with everything, it's not so much *what* is happening to you as it is how you *feel* about it, what your personal experience of it is.

As I said earlier, Chinese medicine defines Earth energy as having to do with the theme of "Mother," so issues with your relationship with your mother can also come up for clearing in this field. (The theme of "Father" is connected to Metal energy, the sixth field.) It's your mother who first teaches you the language of relationships, of how to give and receive in healthy ways. If there were difficult experiences with her in your early life, they can reverberate through your adult relationships. And if there is still discomfort in your current relationship with your mother, or stress held in your system about her even though she's no longer alive, clearing the Earth field can address this.

Clearing the Earth Field

Check your pendulum over your palm to make sure you're not switched, and then take your palm away and silently ask if there is anything to clear in the Earth field. If you get a "yes," then clear.

As always, pay attention to your feelings or anything that comes to mind; don't assume it has nothing to do with what you're clearing. You may discover while discussing the session with your friend that it did have to do with them in some way.

Of course, if you get a "no," there's nothing to clear here, so just skip this field and move on to the sixth.

❀

Sixth Field: Metal
(Life Purpose, Authenticity, Recovering from Loss)

The last field is the Metal Element. The following are some common themes in what may come up for clearing in the Metal field.

Life Purpose

Each of us has a soul's contract, a calling we're striving to answer throughout our life journey. Your purpose can include your career, but it's also about more than what you do for a living. For some people, their job is only meant to supply the financial means to allow them to devote themselves to their calling outside of "work" hours.

We're often unaware that what's on our plate at any current moment is exactly what we need to be working on in order to achieve our purpose. Instead, we just want to eradicate our current problems, thinking they're what are blocking us from what's really important. Instead, we need to recognize that our so-called problems are actually the stepping-stones that are showing the way and helping us evolve so we can fulfill our true calling.

What often comes up to be released in this field are any issues that are preventing you from moving toward your life purpose. Blocks in your external world, such as another person's judgment or beliefs about you, could fall away as a result of the clearing, and then you suddenly get a promotion or job offer. Or in an online search, you might serendipitously stumble across an upcoming workshop that's the exact next step for your own personal evolution.

Clearing this field also addresses internal obstacles to fulfilling your purpose, and one frequent struggle is with that critical inner voice. Patterns of perfectionism or self-criticism can run in the back of your mind like a subliminal radio station constantly broadcasting the message *You're not good enough.* Until you can transform issues of self-worth, you won't be able to reach the very necessary place of genuine pride in who you are becoming. This is not egotistical pride but rather the sense of personal power we all need to claim as we reach each new level of evolution in our lives.

In Chinese medicine, this field also has to do with the theme of "Father," and one aspect of this pattern can relate to your childhood experience of him. Issues from your past relationship with your father may release when this field is cleared, but it can be about even more than that. Your father is the one who's meant to transmit to you a sense of personal power and authority in your life. If he was distant or absent or if he withheld praise, then in your adult life that ancient yearning to make your father proud of you will show up as issues with your own self-worth, a lack of feeling complete within yourself. That can directly affect how well you progress into your life purpose. So clearing this field affects far more than healing childhood issues with your father.

This part of your energy also relates to what Chinese medicine calls "Heaven," or the sky. If you're looking down at your life from up above, you can see the big picture and more easily decide what's most important and valuable to focus on at this point in time. Clearing this field can improve your ability to hold an open awareness and see the long view. It's with this frame of mind that you can truly fulfill your soul's contract.

Authenticity

Another meaning to "Heaven" is to feel a sense of the sacred in your life. This can mean being a spiritual person, but it can also have to do with feeling free to live your truth, to be authentic. If you struggle with self-worth or perfectionism, this can cause such a sense of anguish, as if living authentically always seems just out of reach. Clearing in this field can bring a dawning of a new awareness, that you actually *are* good enough exactly as you are right now.

When you can reach a place of knowing there really is nothing missing, that you're not inherently lacking as a person, then you can finally feel comfortable in your own skin and be your authentic self. This kind of release can bring you to a place where you feel back on track in life.

Although a sense of such an open awareness is beneficial, there's also a downside. Clearing in this field is so valuable for people who are highly sensitive because they're *too* wide open. In this case, it means they're physically affected by the energy of the people and places around them. You can be highly sensitive because you were born that way, or you can become highly sensitive because of life experiences that have made you so. Either way, you may have what Chinese medicine calls "thin skin," the tendency to too easily absorb the energy around you. The result can be frequent overwhelm and even somatic reactions such as physical discomfort, allergies, or environmental sensitivities.

This can lead to a constant undercurrent of anxiety. It can make you keep your life too small because you are fearful of taking risks, or you may avoid social situations in trying to prevent overwhelm. This can cause misunderstandings with others who may misinterpret your coping mechanisms and judge you as standoffish, or too controlling, needing everything your way. What they don't understand is that these are just your attempts to manage your experience. Further, when you feel criticized by others, it's impossible to feel like you have permission to be your authentic self.

Clearing in this field can help you develop better boundaries so you're no longer taking on the energy around you. Your system can then become more robust and better able to move through the world without feeling under assault by all the invisible information coming at you. It can awaken your ability to be more true to your nature because when you're no longer spending energy contending with everything around you, you can turn your attention to yourself.

Recovering from Loss

Chinese medicine describes the emotion associated with this field as "grief." The full concept, however, embraces much more than someone dying or the loss of a love relationship, which is usually how people define grief in their minds. What can come up to be cleared in this field has to do with *any* losses you've experienced in your life and where you are in the process of recovering, letting go, and moving on.

Each of us is unique in how we go through the grief process, and there are no rules about how long it takes for us to emerge at the other end of that journey. However, it's not uncommon to get stalled at some point along the way. Some people repeatedly look back with regret about the loss and torture themselves with how they might have prevented it or done things better. The regrets can be endless: *If only I hadn't said that. If only I had tried harder . . . been a better person . . . listened to my intuition . . .*

Clearing here can help you look back less and less often; instead, you'll turn to face forward and focus on using what you learned from the past experience to add quality to your future. Then when you do look back, it's with a sense of profound gratitude for how you were enriched by that part of your life, even including the loss, because it made you a deeper, wiser, and stronger person.

Clearing this field also affects your ability to let go in other ways. If you're struggling with a loss, you can be afraid of letting yourself really feel your grief. You may believe that the feelings would be so intense, you'd be overwhelmed and unable to cope. Or you may view grieving as a sign of weakness, and so cut yourself off from your feelings and try to just get on with life. But this never works; there is always a hole in your spirit. No situation exists in isolation, so if you try to avoid your emotions, your energy contracts in other ways as well. As you control your feelings, you can become more and more rigid, more distant with others, and more cut off from your joy; eventually, even your health could be affected.

Grief must be honored. The process of grief is one that leads you to a place you can't imagine when you're lost in the pain. The gift that comes after you allow your grief is the recognition of how much you've actually gained—not despite the loss but because of it.

Clearing the Metal Field

Again, make sure you're still in balance, and then ask if there is anything to clear in the Metal field. If you get a "yes," proceed. If you get a "no," just move on to the next step: integration.

Remember to trust the answers the pendulum gives you and to pay attention to even the most fleeting of impressions. Assume it has something to do with the clearing even if you don't understand it.

❀

The Two Final Steps of the Clearing

Once you've cleared the Metal field, there are no more personal energy fields to clear, but there are two final steps before you're done: integration and grounding. This is because, although it often looks like nothing is happening during a clearing, there's actually deep and significant change occurring invisibly. The person's energy has been moving, shifting, releasing, and processing. It's important to create an opportunity for the changes to integrate within their system on every level, and to then ground the person to make sure you leave them feeling complete and centered in their body and spirit.

Integration and grounding are always necessary steps, so there's no need to ask if they need to be done, the way you do when clearing the six previous fields.

Integration

Start by simply letting your pendulum swing just like it does when you're clearing. This time, hold in mind that you're allowing whatever integration is necessary to happen; continue until the pendulum indicates the process is complete.

You should not try to *make* the other person's energy integrate; don't visualize some result or intend some specific change. Doing so would be forcing the process, which would immediately bring things to a halt. Just tell yourself that integration is happening. Trust that when it's complete, the pendulum will let you know.

If you can do this, you're staying present. Then, not only will the integration be successful, but you may also feel it as it happens, which can be quite a lovely experience.

Grounding

To allow grounding, simply hold your pendulum and go into clearing mode as usual. Remember, you don't have to do anything to *make* it happen. Just hold the thought in mind that their system is "grounding" and stay aware of what you feel as the pendulum swings. With some people, you may notice a pleasant sort of *whump!* sensation as they ground quickly and easily, and you'll see the pendulum change motion to let you know you're done. With others, you may not feel anything, or you may sense that it's not so easy for them to get grounded. In that case, this step may take a while before the pendulum signals that this last part of the session is finished.

❦

Congratulations—you've now completed the clearing! In the next chapter, we'll discuss what you should do after a clearing and what's most important for you to know from here.

chapter 6

After the Clearing

---

advice, answers
& reminders

You now know how to do a personal clearing. You've learned the preliminary steps to take beforehand and how to do the full clearing, all the way through integration and grounding. Now, in this chapter, we'll go over how and when to have a discussion about any feelings that came up during a session, how you might feel after doing a clearing or having one done for you, and what might unfold in your life afterward as a result.

Finally, I'll end the chapter with advice about what to keep in mind during a clearing and answers to the most frequently asked questions I hear in my workshops. I also include a step-by-step how-to list you can refer to when you do a clearing for someone.

Sharing Your Feelings and Impressions

When it comes to having a conversation about what you felt while you were clearing your friend, you have two options: You can pause between each field while you're doing the clearing and discuss the thoughts, emotions, sensations, or impressions that you each had while it's still fresh in your minds. Or, if you prefer, you can complete the entire clearing, and then once you're done, sit and quietly share about what came up.

Your friend may say they had some feelings similar to yours, or that something you said made sense to them in ways you couldn't possibly have known. That can be a confidence booster for you. For instance, perhaps you mention that you felt some heavy feelings of worry pass through your awareness during the clearing, and they respond that they're not surprised to hear that because they're so concerned about an urgent family problem right now. You might have felt some waves of exhaustion, only to have them report that they're struggling with chronic fatigue.

Some people have old memories come up while they're being cleared, things they haven't thought about in years but relate to the impressions you were getting in some of the fields. This is because, when you do a clearing, you're connecting with their entire life history, not just the stresses of the moment. In so many ways, it can be valuable for both of you to compare what you felt or thought during the session.

Even if nothing you felt seems to make sense to the other person, it doesn't mean you weren't connected to their energy. Much of what we feel during a clearing can have to do with how our own systems are sensing the information. So if you felt a twinge in your shoulder, but they say they've never had a problem with their shoulder, it can simply be that this was just how you experienced the energy moving.

Remember that it's also common for the other person to feel nothing at all as you clear them. Clearing is a subtle process, and most people aren't used to being aware of fleeting thoughts or feelings. And if *you* didn't sense anything while you cleared, remember that you're still learning. Much of your attention will be on recalling what to do when, and how to drive this pendulum-thingy! As you practice doing more clearings, you'll start to notice sensations, emotions, or impressions; it just takes time to work at that level.

How Someone May Feel after Being Cleared

During your conversation at the end of the clearing, it's helpful to briefly explain to your friend how they may feel in the hours afterward. For instance, it's normal to be mildly relaxed, like you might feel after a massage, and to want to have some quiet time alone. Another standard reaction is to become tired and crave a nap. However, it's also common to feel exhilarated and energized. I've had people feel so revitalized after a clearing that they cleaned their house from top to bottom or created a complete new business plan!

Alternatively, they may feel a little unsettled for a while as they get used to the changes in their energy. It's normal to occasionally have an emotional release after a clearing, so they might have a good cry or an upset with their spouse. This is not at all a bad sign! Remember the image of a garden hose with a kink in it—when you unkink that hose, the water might spurt out dramatically as it's finally released after having built up a lot of pressure. In the same way, there can sometimes be a surge of energy as a result of a clearing due to feelings being stuck, suppressed, or unspoken for such a long time. After that initial release, things smooth out and there can be remarkable new developments from there.

How You May Feel after Doing a Clearing

After doing a clearing, you might feel so much better yourself, like *you've* also been cleared, and that's not your imagination! When you do a clearing, energy is moving for you as well, and this is one of the reasons people love to do this work. So don't be surprised if you feel exhilarated and like you're walking on air!

It's also not unusual to feel very peaceful, quiet, and in touch with your feelings afterward. Sometimes, you may feel tired, and this can be due to your own system relaxing and allowing you to *feel* for the first time the tiredness that's actually been in your life for a while. If we push too hard in our own lives, we tend to suppress how tired we are so we can keep going, but this isn't a healthy way to live. At the extreme, it's like the person who's so stressed out that they get sick on their first day of vacation. This is what Western medicine calls the "letdown effect": when someone gets sick *after* a stressful period, when they're finally beginning to unwind. They've been holding it all together for so long that the moment their body gets a chance to relax, everything falls in on itself. So the clearing may not be what makes you tired; instead, it allowed you to sink into your own feelings for the first time in a while and notice what's really going on for you.

However, sometimes the reason you feel in need of rest *is* due to your just having done a clearing. You've been connecting with another person's energy fields, feeling things shift and move during the process, and you're still getting used to that experience. It can take some effort at first as you practice a new level of awareness, sensing the energy and tuning in to intuitive impressions. After you've been doing this work for a while, this all becomes more and more effortless.

If you do feel too tired or unsettled after a clearing, it can be because you were trying too hard. For one thing, as a beginner, it's completely normal for you to think you're not doing enough. Your brain tells you that just watching a pendulum swing and paying attention to your feelings couldn't possibly have any effect! It can be hard to understand that there are actually invisible yet powerful shifts happening as you do this because of the energetic exchange between you and the other person. So instead of trusting the process and allowing the clearing to take place naturally, you may try too hard, or push a bit energetically to be sure you do a good job! But that means you're trying to *do* something, rather than to *be* with the energy presenting. And if you're "doing" something, that *does* take effort. So you not only end up tired but also the clearing won't have been very effective.

Another reason you may unintentionally try to "do" something is if you have an attachment to a certain outcome. It's easy to fall into this because you so earnestly want to help your friend. It's also possible that as a consequence of your sincere desire to help, you might unconsciously try to take some of their stress and end up carrying it home with you and that will definitely make you feel tired! (These are things that happen only to beginners; once you get more practice, they won't occur.)

But experiences like these are easily resolved. First of all, any feelings of tiredness or being unsettled will naturally fade after a bit of a rest, a hearty meal, or a good night's sleep. It can also help to clear yourself or to reach out and ask someone to clear you. This is why the online community is so wonderful; someone is always awake in the world to see your request and do a clearing for you. (You can find this resource at www.facebook.com/clearhomeclearheart.)

Results of a Clearing

Sometimes there's an almost magical result imme-diately after a clearing. One time, the phone rang the moment the session was over—it was my client's sister, who hadn't spoken to her in 20 years, calling to ask to heal their relationship. I've done clearings where the very next day, my client was offered a multimillion-dollar contract or had a lawsuit that had been dragging on for years sud-denly resolved in their favor.

Other times, the results unfold after a series of clear-ings and in unexpected ways. My client Sarah had sched-uled three monthly sessions because she hoped to bring better relationships into her life. The day after her third clearing, she learned her mother was coming for a visit for the first time in years. Sarah was apprehensive because her mother was a very negative, critical woman, and any time spent with her had always left Sarah extremely stressed and upset. But a few days after the visit was over, she e-mailed me to say it had been like a miracle. From the first moment her mother walked through the door, Sarah didn't brace herself for an onslaught of negativity. Instead, she said, "I saw her as just a person. It was like I no longer had the baggage of the past to deal with, and I could see her with-out the old filter of pain and hurt." To the amazement of both of them, they spent the week together sightseeing, eating out, and laughing. Sarah said, "I realized that it had been my relationship with my mother that first had to be cleared before I could attract better relationships overall."

You can never predict the results of a clearing because you don't know what has to clear first in order for some-thing else to be released, or how or when the shifts need to happen. Don't assume that you know what has to occur in order for balance to be returned to the situation.

For instance, a client of mine had a dog who became very ill, and she contacted me for a clearing for him, hoping that it would ease his suffering or possibly even heal him. Although her vet said she had to see a specialist immediately, that office was booked for weeks and couldn't squeeze her in. The best she could do was to get on the long list of people waiting for a cancellation.

One hour after I finished the clearing, her phone rang; it was the specialist's office. They'd just had a cancellation, and none of the people ahead of her on the waiting list could make it, so the appointment was hers. Wonderfully, that vet was able to return her dog to health, and he said that if she'd waited any longer, the dog wouldn't have survived. So although the clearing didn't result in a healing as my client had hoped, it may have opened up an appointment so he could be healed!

Sometimes a clearing shows us that what we think we want is not what's right for us after all. One woman had hoped that a clearing would result in her fiancé finally setting a date for their wedding. What happened instead was that he ran off with another woman and later was arrested and charged with embezzlement! My client realized that if they'd gotten married, this could have severely affected her own financial safety, and she felt the clearing had saved her from that devastating experience.

It's possible for just one clearing to create a huge shift that frees you from a major life issue; other times, a series of clearings is needed to gently peel away the layers. Changes can start with small issues disappearing in surprising ways. You may not even notice the effects until you look back over what's happened in your life since the clearing, and then you can trace the results that took place one after the other, like dominoes falling.

Remember, as you go through your days, you can take on new stress that you can't always successfully let go of by yourself. I usually suggest that people get a clearing once a week, in person or remotely, from someone who's also learned this work. With each session, more of the tension and stress you've been carrying will release, and a new coherence will begin to appear, a harmonious and vibrant flow of energy throughout your spirit and your life.

Important Dos and Don'ts for Personal Clearing

You've just taken in a *lot* of information. What I've found in all my years of teaching this work is that at this stage, it's really helpful to have a bit of a review, as well as some essential advice about some important things to keep in mind that otherwise might get overlooked as you try to integrate what you're learning. So here are some dos and don'ts to remember:

DO check between each field. Before you start to clear each subsequent field, it's always helpful to briefly swing the pendulum over your palm just to check whether you're still in balance. This is because there might have been something in the last field you tuned in to that triggered an old memory or stress in your *own* system, and so your energy got switched. This doesn't happen very often, but checking is a helpful habit to cultivate just in case.

If you find you've become switched, it's usually enough to just take a deep breath to rebalance. Then when you check again, you'll see the pendulum returns to its normal movement over your palm. If it doesn't, it's not a problem. Just follow the advice on page 33 for what to do when you're switched.

So, for example, when the pendulum indicates you're done clearing Disturbing Effects of Others, before you move on to ask about the Water field, hold the pendulum over your palm for a moment just to see if it swings as it should. If it does, then take your palm away and continue on to ask about that next field.

DO maintain rapport. When you're first learning, you probably won't be able to carry on much of a conversation while you're clearing someone. You'll be too focused on holding the thought in mind, paying attention to what you're feeling, and watching your pendulum. But this means you're not maintaining much eye contact with your friend, let alone talking to them! So they might end up sitting there feeling quite alone and wondering what's going on.

In order to maintain rapport, be sure to look up now and then and smile, tell them when each field is almost done, or in some way make sure they know you're there for them. After you clear each field, you might want to pause and talk about any sensations or impressions you had or discuss anything they want to share.

As you start to clear each new field, it can help to say a sentence or two about what this field is usually about. This gives your friend a sense of what you're tuning in to and makes them feel more engaged. For instance, as you start to clear the Water field, you might say, "In this field, what sometimes comes up to clear are any issues where fear is blocking you." It does *not* mean you have to focus on clearing their "fear"; you just hold in mind that you're clearing Water and pay attention to what you feel. A comment like that is to help give them a foundation for what may be happening so they don't feel lost, and it can also give them an opening to tell you about a current issue in their life where they know fear is blocking them from moving forward. It also simply helps them relax more so the clearing is even more effective.

Although at first it can be hard to talk and clear at the same time, it just takes practice. After you've had more experience, you'll be able to carry on a back-and-forth conversation throughout the clearing with no problem. However, as you talk during the session, respect your friend's privacy and comfort level and don't push them to share. Some people appreciate the chance to talk about what's going on in their life before you do the clearing, during it, or afterward. But others may be reluctant to open up and of course you'll honor that.

It's also essential to never make someone feel as if they're supposed to have some dramatic experience or instant results during the clearing! Avoid questions like, "Are you feeling better?" or anything else that could make them feel like you have expectations for them. And remember, don't feel discouraged if they don't report noticing anything during the clearing. Most people are not used to being aware of small or subtle feelings.

DO allow a yawn and keep tissues handy. It's not unusual to experience any of three reactions when you do a clearing: yawning, nose running, or eyes tearing. In qi gong (the ancient Chinese energy healing practice), these are classic symptoms of the system detoxifying. In fact, more than one qi gong master has said that clearing is like the highest level of qi gong.

What's happening is that you've connected with the other person's energy—you're feeling their stress as it clears, and this reaction can occur to help that process. So don't be concerned if any of these things happen when you do a clearing. You may have to reassure the person you're clearing that your yawn doesn't mean you're bored—you're just releasing their negativity!

DON'T attempt to diagnose their health. I don't care if you firmly believe you got a message that there's something wrong with their stomach and they should see a doctor immediately. Unless you are a medical professional and can give them a physical examination, or are a highly trained medical intuitive, you should *never* try to diagnose health issues.

If you felt something in a part of your body, then you can share that with them. Always remember, however, that this could simply be how your system is experiencing the information that's clearing, and it may have nothing to do with the other person at all, much less their health. If they can't relate to what you say, make sure to explain this to them. Even if they say they previously had a health issue in that part of their body, it may mean you were clearing any imbalances remaining there; don't assume the previous health problem has recurred.

DON'T make promises about results. Once you've experienced this work and the feeling of peace and well-being it brings, it can be tempting to start off a clearing by telling someone, "This will make you feel much better." In the long run, it definitely will, but what first may need to happen is that their suppressed unhappiness emerges in a big fight with their spouse!

Sometimes difficult things have to be said or uncomfortable feelings have to be processed in order for positive change to happen. But if you promised them "love and light," they're going to think you didn't do a good job clearing them, or that something went wrong. In fact, your clearing may have been exceptionally powerful and it will help them move beyond their stuck places, but first there are some necessary surges and bumps as the energy transforms. Sometimes people do feel amazingly wonderful right after a clearing, but if they don't, that doesn't mean it wasn't effective.

DON'T have an attachment to a specific outcome. This is so important. We never know what needs to clear in order for balance and well-being to return to someone's life. Additionally, if we think we have to achieve a certain outcome with a clearing, we may miss something even more wonderful that can happen as a result. We have such a tiny keyhole view of what's going on at any one time. We like to think we can figure out what's best, and we assume things work in straight lines, a cause-and-effect process; but, in fact, Life is more beautifully complex and mysterious than that!

At times, it can be hard to not be attached to an outcome. If the person you're clearing is suffering with the flu, you want them to feel better as a result of your work. In fact, a clearing often does ease discomfort when someone is ill, and sometimes they actually do get better right after a session. But alternatively, it might be that the time at home recovering is exactly what they need in order to realize they should make some new choices in life. If they'd gotten better and went right back to work, they would have missed that opportunity for positive change. If that's the case, then the clearing will support their staying home in bed so that "aha!" can happen.

If someone desperately wants to get that promotion, you can get caught up in hoping the clearing creates that result. But it could be that if they got the promotion, they'd be caught in a hamster wheel of work and anxiety, and all that extra money they were earning would be spent on therapists' and doctors' bills because they were so stressed!

Trying to help make things all better, projecting your perceptions of what you believe is "good" for someone, or getting lost in your own emotions about the situation all interfere with your effectiveness. Just breathe, stay present, be aware of your feelings but don't get swept away in them, and clear.

Frequently Asked Questions (FAQs)

There are common questions I get at this point in the training, so on the following pages you'll find some answers to topics you may have been wanting to ask about!

"What if I don't have time to do a full personal clearing?"

Although ideally you'll do a full clearing, working through each of the fields and ending with integration and grounding, sometimes it's simply not possible. Perhaps a friend needs your clearing help but you have only a few minutes to spare. In that case, you can do what's called a general clearing.

First, you check to make sure you're not switched. Then ask if it's appropriate to proceed; if you get a "yes," just give your pendulum a swing to get it going, and let yourself drop into what I call the feeling you'll be more and more familiar with: clearing mode.

Tell yourself that you are setting the time for the session to be five minutes (or whatever amount of time you have) and hold the thought in mind that you're clearing your friend. You don't have to go through the individual fields. The pendulum will make its usual clearing movement and will indicate when it's done, which is almost always within the time frame you set.

However, I don't suggest you do any general clearings until you've had plenty of practice doing full clearings because you simply won't have enough experience to be very focused or effective. And again, it's always best to do a full clearing rather than a general one.

"How often should someone get a clearing?"

I recommend having a clearing once a week, but any time you feel especially stressed by your day, don't hesitate to get one or to clear yourself!

One of the nice things about this system is that you can work with a partner and exchange personal clearings on a regular basis. You can do this with friends who have also read this book or have been to a workshop, or you can turn to the beautiful, caring community that's grown up around this work by going to www.facebook.com /clearhomeclearheart to find a clearing partner.

You can clear your partner in person, or while you're together on the phone or a video chat. You can also clear them alone, at your own convenience, and then simply e-mail them, send them a private message, or call them about it later. However, I recommend not working with any one partner for more than three months at a time because you can get too used to each other's energy and therefore be less effective. It's also great training for you to work with a new partner every few months— you'll see how different the experience is with each person's energy!

"At what point can I start clearing myself?"

You can practice clearing yourself right now. However, until you've had good experience clearing others, you won't be able to clear much of your own "stuff." You're too close, too used to your own energy, and haven't yet developed your understanding of the work in a way that you get only through clearing others. So when you clear yourself at this early stage, you might clear only 10 percent of what's able to be released at that time, while another person would be able to clear 80 percent for you!

Later on, once you've built your skills with this work, you'll be able to clear yourself beautifully. At that point, I recommend even doing it on a daily basis if that feels right to you. Eventually, you'll just be naturally clearing yourself as you go through your day. You'll be letting go of stressed thoughts and feelings as they arise without having to pull out your pendulum or work through the fields. It will become automatic—whenever you encounter stress, you clear it!

"Can I clear someone if I'm sick?"

It's probably best to wait until you're better. But if you follow the protocol, you'll find this out yourself because there are safeguards built into these methods. If you're too sick to do a clearing, your pendulum may show that you're switched, and you won't be able to get yourself back into balance with the usual techniques. Or when you ask if it's appropriate to proceed, you'll get a "no." Or you'll start clearing, but as you ask if there's anything to clear in each field, you keep getting "no."

Understand that one of the benefits of this work is that it puts you in touch with your feelings. Listen to your body. If you don't feel well enough to do a clearing, then don't. It doesn't matter if your friend is in distress and you feel guilty about not helping. Pushing yourself to do something that's not right for you comes from an unhealthy emotional place, not a balanced one.

If you've listened to your feelings and still want to try, and the pendulum gives you the appropriate go-ahead, then it's probably fine. Doing a clearing for someone also benefits your energy, so you'll often feel much better as a result of clearing someone else.

"Can you clear babies and children? Can I teach my child how to clear?"

You can clear any living being. I love when parents come to my workshops because they often report afterward what an amazing experience it is to clear their own children, and how their kids now come to them to ask for a clearing when they're upset.

However, I do not recommend that you try to teach your child how to clear. For one thing, they don't yet have the emotional maturity to understand the process. Something very important to remember is that children are extremely sensitive to energy but haven't yet learned how to manage any of that sensitivity. If you teach them how to deliberately open to stressed energy, it can be too much for them. They'll naturally feel more than an adult will because they've not had the decades of gradually shutting down that most adults need to undo!

Some parents see their highly sensitive child struggling to manage their everyday experience in the world and so want to teach them clearing in order to help them cope. If you're in this situation, know that there are positive and powerful alternatives you can teach them that can really help at this stage in their life. I've posted some for you at www.jeanhaner.com/highlysensitivechildren.

Depending on a child's individual maturity, I'd suggest waiting until they're in their midteens before getting them interested in learning *how* to clear. Until then, just allow them to enjoy the benefits of *being* cleared!

❦

Now you've followed me through the process of doing a personal clearing and have developed a basic understanding of what to do. On the next page, you'll find a checklist that can help you easily remember each step.

CHECKLIST FOR A PERSONAL CLEARING

Here's an abbreviated step-by-step guide to refer to when you do a personal clearing. Please don't use this shorthand version until you've read and understood the full information covered in Part I.

1. Holding the pendulum over your palm, check to make sure you're not switched.

2. Take a deep breath, relax, and become aware of your feelings.

3. Ask: "Is it appropriate to proceed?" If "yes," continue; if "no," try the clearing at another time.

4. Tell the person you're clearing to relax and just be aware of what they feel or anything that comes to mind during the session so you can discuss it later on.

5. Hold a calm, open "passive wondering" state of mind.

6. Ask: "Is there anything to clear in Disturbing Effects of Others?" If "yes," clear. If "no," you most likely are switched or unable to clear at this time. Refer to page 33 for what to do.

7. Ask: "Is there anything to clear in Water?" If "yes," clear; if "no," continue on to ask about the next field.

8. Ask: "Is there anything to clear in Wood?" If "yes," clear; if "no," continue on to ask about the next field.

9. Ask: "Is there anything to clear in Fire?" If "yes," clear; if "no," continue on to ask about the next field.

10. Ask: "Is there anything to clear in Earth?" If "yes," clear; if "no," continue on to ask about the next field.

11. Ask: "Is there anything to clear in Metal?" If "yes," clear; if "no," continue on to do the next two steps.

12. Clear for Integration.

13. Clear for Grounding.

14. End with a quiet conversation with the other person, sharing what you each may have thought about, felt, or sensed as you worked. Explain how they might feel in the hours afterward.

NOTE: You can watch a brief demonstration of a clearing at www.jeanhaner.com/clearingvideos.

Congratulations—you've learned how to bring a person's energy back into balance! But remember, it's not just people that can carry stress. Each of us lives and works in places that can hold stuck or imbalanced energy that can affect how we feel there. So now we turn to clearing the energy of environments!

part II

SPACE
CLEARING

❦ ❦ ❦

Your house is your larger body.

— Kahlil Gibran

chapter 7

Emotions Can
Linger in a Space

One of the very first professional space clearings I did was for Monique, a single woman in a severely cluttered bungalow. There were so many belongings stacked everywhere that she could open the front door only a crack to let me in, and we had to navigate narrow paths in the hallways to squeeze between the piles and boxes.

My first thought as I entered was, *This is ridiculous. This woman doesn't need a space clearing. She needs someone to pull a gigantic Dumpster up to her house and shovel all this stuff out.* I tried to talk her out of the clearing, saying that I thought her first step should be to bring in an organizer to deal with the clutter, and then I'd be happy to come back to do the space clearing. I didn't want to take her money for something that would have little effect. But Monique insisted, saying she'd considered that but her intuition told her this was the necessary first step. So we sat down and I asked about what her experience there had been.

Monique told me that she and her husband had bought the house seven years ago, right after they were married. They'd gotten a great deal because it had been a run-down rental house previously occupied by a motorcycle gang. In fact, the neighbors informed her that there'd been such violent fights at the house, the police were often called in to break them up!

Within a few months of moving in, Monique and her husband began arguing more frequently, and then he started hitting her. He'd never acted this way before, but he became increasingly physical with her. After three years, the marriage ended in divorce. Since that time, she'd fallen into depression, and the clutter began to grow. So unhappy in her job that she could barely force herself to go to work each day, she craved a new direction but felt stuck and hopeless.

The energy in the house was palpably heavy; it was like trying to walk underwater. As I did the space clearing, I felt shifts in the flow but was still doubtful this would have much impact, considering all the clutter crammed in every room. At the end, I did a personal clearing for Monique as well, and I felt her sincere desire to move beyond all this stuckness. Still, I left that day feeling guilty that I'd let her pay me anything because I couldn't imagine my work would have much impact.

Two weeks later, she called me and said, "Jean, I just had to let you know what happened after your clearing. The very next morning, my doorbell rang and there stood my two best friends, and in the driveway was one of those huge industrial Dumpsters. They said they couldn't stand seeing me or my house this way anymore, so they'd paid to have the Dumpster brought in, and they were going to help me shovel out my house!"

So my very first impression as I arrived, which I had never mentioned to Monique, immediately manifested after the clearing! She went on to tell me that a few days after emptying out her house, she bought a lottery ticket on a whim and won $25,000. The next day, she realized what she really wanted to do was be a massage therapist, and this money would let her quit her job and go to school. She was actually calling me on the way to the airport because she was giving herself a celebratory vacation in Hawaii first!

Talk about energy moving! What most likely had happened is that the disturbed energy of the former renters influenced how she and her husband felt in the space, creating an atmosphere that supported arguments, if not worse. The clutter that had built up was a visual reflection of the thick fog of emotions that had accumulated in the space from the gang members' personalities as well as Monique and her husband's problems, let alone whoever had lived in the house previously.

Of course, we can never know for sure if the space clearing had any part in her transformation, but I've seen so many seemingly "magical" breakthroughs like this over the years that I've come to trust this work. It's not about magic but simply how effortlessly things can unfold once the energy returns to balance.

And that's what space clearing is all about. Just like a personal clearing brings an individual's energy fields back into balance, the same thing can be done for an environment.

The Residue of Emotions Left in Your Space Affects How You Feel There

The energy of your surroundings affects you on many levels. Over time, in any building, the qi (energy) can become stagnant or stressed. When that happens, it can keep you stuck in life or be a detrimental influence on you mentally, emotionally, and even physically.

One thing that could make the energy in a space become this way is the accumulated effect of the thoughts and emotions you have as you live there. Each time you have a feeling, you make a little imprint of that vibration in your environment. Over time, these gradually build up to form layers of energetic residue, like invisible house dust, that then begin to affect how easily the qi can move through the space.

When energy can't flow freely, stagnation occurs, and your own energy can start to become sluggish as well. Physically, it could make you feel increasingly lethargic. Mentally, it can interfere with your clarity of mind. Emotionally, it can block your natural optimism and can even contribute to depression. Stagnation in your space can be part of why you feel stuck in life overall.

Your feelings get imprinted in your surroundings. The thoughts and feelings you have just in the course of your normal daily life are enough to build up and eventually block the qi flow. But the quality of those vibrations also matter. If you have repeated feelings of anxiety and worry, or frequent negative and self-defeating thoughts, those don't just affect your inner world. They set up a resonance in your outer world as well and increase the likelihood that you'll get locked into feeling like that again each time you're in the space.

For example, when I'm doing a space clearing, I often find an area of stressed energy in front of the kitchen sink. This is where people often stand for a while as they prepare a meal or put dishes in the dishwasher and, at the same time, run that repeating loop of rumination inside their heads. It may be frustration with their spouse, or worry about their child, or resentment about co-workers, or all of the above and then some. People often tend to think about the same issues day after day, week after week, so an invisible fog holding that information gradually develops in that spot. Then every time they stand there, they're triggered to have those same feelings again, like a vicious cycle.

So as you live your everyday life, you repeatedly broadcast those same vibrations out into your environment and alter its energy. And if you have an intense experience, such as a heated argument or an upset in a certain spot in the house, it can embed that one feeling there. Even though it may have been a single event, if the magnitude of the emotion felt there is powerful enough, it can linger to affect you each time you're in that place again.

For instance, Leah had a horrible fight with her boyfriend as he broke up with her. It took place as they sat on her living room couch, and from that point on, every time she was on the couch, she'd melt into tears as feelings of sadness and betrayal overwhelmed her. Because Leah's habit was to head for the couch after dinner, she was spending every evening lost in her pain, far more so than if she wasn't sitting in the spot where the breakup happened. It was keeping her locked in to reexperiencing the original shock and hurt.

When I cleared Leah's house, the anguish held in the couch was acute. I wasn't surprised to then hear her explain what had happened there. But I felt the painful feelings clear beautifully, and Leah reported afterward that she could now sit on the couch without any tears coming. In fact, she felt her heart was healing enough that she was about to have her first date since the breakup.

Previous Occupants' Energy Also Leaves Invisible Clutter

So your stress can build up in your environment like invisible clutter, but the energy from past occupants of a space can also leave a residue there as well. Who lived in your house before you? Did they have a difficult relationship that could have left negativity lingering there to affect how *your* marriage goes? Was someone an emotional eater, leaving the imprints of their constant cravings in the house, which can then influence your own discipline with food? You have your own problems—why live in a house infused with the issues of the previous owners too?

One space clearing I did exemplified how this residual energy can affect businesses as well as homes. I was brought in by a company that had grown so fast, they had to move into a new, larger headquarters much earlier than expected. They told me they attributed their quick success to the warm and supportive relationships among the staff. Everyone felt such a camaraderie together—until they landed in these new offices. Then, they said, people suddenly started "stabbing each other in the back," and "staff meetings turned into bloodbaths." Business took a nosedive as a result.

When I arrived to do the space clearing, I could tell that management was immediately relieved to see that I showed up in a suit and heels, carrying a clipboard. (I think they half-expected me to wear veils and dance around with incense!) The nice thing about doing this work is that once you're proficient, you can simply walk through a place and clear it without anyone knowing. So instead of employees wondering what the heck is going on, I can be introduced as a "space planner" if necessary. I walk around with my clipboard, making notes as if planning a new interior design; in fact, I'm actually clearing imbalances as I sense them. And, wow, was I sensing them there from the moment I arrived!

This company's century-old building was full of energetic disturbances, far more than I'd expect even for such an old place. I sat down for a brief interview with the CEO and asked if he knew what the building had been used for prior to their moving in. He said, "Oh yeah, it used to be a pig slaughterhouse. If you look under the rug, you'll find the channels they carved into the floor to let the blood flow out. We just put down the carpeting, brought in the desks, and got to work!" *Oh my.* So the decades upon decades of knives, blood, fear, and death had left a deep imprint, creating a psychic atmosphere supporting "backstabbing" and "bloodbaths"! Fortunately, this energy cleared surprisingly easily; as often happens, it felt to me as if the stress was yearning to be released.

The greater the length of time that emotions are felt repeatedly in the space—whether it's due to the experience of violence or, more commonly, just your own daily stresses and anxieties—the more the energy will lose its healthy flow. If you move into a brand-new house, there will be little of this buildup. Sure, some of the construction workers' personal "stuff" might remain, and perhaps a little of the real estate agents' or potential buyers' qi could linger there. However, because these weren't people relaxing and sinking into their private feelings as people do at home, there won't be much residue. But if you move into a house that had previous owners, or if you've lived in your home for more than a few years, there are layers and layers of "psychic house dust" that can stress your system or tire you out. And if there's a history of more traumatic experiences in a building, the people in the space will be more severely affected, as was the case with the business in the old slaughterhouse.

The imprint of the emotions experienced in your surroundings is one important aspect that we work with in an energy clearing. So let's move on to see how to clear the energy in a space!

chapter 8

How to Clear the Residue of Emotions Held in a Space

When you first start a space clearing, it can be helpful to just get a general "read" on the overall quality of the energy in the place. You can do this by using your pendulum to check on how much "yin" energy and how much "yang" there is in the space as a whole.

You may be familiar with the concept of yin and yang, with yin energy being more quiet, internal, still; and yang being more active, external, in motion. There are always both yin and yang qualities to everything, just in different measures. For instance, some people seem more yin: introverted, quiet, and shy. Others appear more yang: extroverted, talkative, and sociable. But all of us and everything in nature have both yin and yang in a certain ratio.

The energy of an environment also has certain amounts of yin and yang. It's the yang energy that gives you the get-up-and-go vitality to leave your bed in the morning and head off to work. The yin energy helps you to relax and rest, as well as stay in touch with your emotional side. In general, the ideal ratio for most homes is about 60 percent yang energy and 40 percent yin because a little more yang energy helps you stay alert and get things done.

However, as you have your daily emotions in the space, the balance of yin and yang in your home can change. Most emotions are yin, which means that as the residue left from your feelings naturally builds up over time, the percentage of yin in the space rises. Instead of 40 percent yin, the environment slowly rises to 45, 50, 55, or 60 percent yin, or more. The result can be that it's harder to get out of bed in the morning, and once you get home at night, all you can do is sink into the couch and watch TV till bedtime. You can feel lethargic, unmotivated, and stuck, and eventually this can support depression or even illness.

It's certainly possible for an environment to be overly yang instead. The two most common causes for this are frequent episodes of intense anger or violence in the space over time, or earth energies that have become stressed. (We'll talk about earth energies in Chapter 9.) If the place has too much yang qi, you may find you can't sit still or relax, or your sleep is disturbed. You might also be working constantly or often get caught up in frustration or anger.

Checking the Balance of Yin and Yang in a Space

So one of the first things we do in a space clearing is use the pendulum to find out what the ratio of yin to yang is in this space. To start, hold your pendulum over your palm to check to see if you're switched. If you're in balance, then ask, "Is the energy in this space more yin than yang?"

If you get a "yes," you then determine just how high the yin percentage is. I find you get the most accurate answer by counting backward until you get a "yes."

For example, ask: "Is it 100 percent yin?" Most likely your pendulum will say "no" because it's virtually impossible for a place to be completely yin! You then continue counting down by 10 until you get a "yes."

"Is it 90 percent or more yin?" "No."
"Is it 80 percent or more yin?" "No."
"Is it 70 percent or more yin?" "No."
"Is it 60 percent or more yin?" "Yes."

So you now know that the yin energy in this place is somewhere between 60 and 70 percent. You don't have to continue on to calculate the exact percentage because that's not really important. Knowing the range is enough to alert you to just how much of the clearing will probably be to release emotional disturbances.

A New Tool to Use for Space Clearing!

In addition to a pendulum, there's a second tool to use in space clearing: a dowsing rod. You may have seen pictures of someone using dowsing rods to look for underground water so they can find the best place to dig a well, but that's not the only way they can be used. A dowsing rod is simply a tool you can use to locate something unseen in an environment. In our work with space clearing, we use a dowsing rod to locate different kinds of energy in a space.

People have been using dowsing rods for thousands of years. Egyptian carvings dating back to the times of the pyramids show images of men dowsing with sticks. There were dowsers in ancient China. In medieval Europe, miners used the rods to find precious metals underground. In modern times, the U.S. military even used dowsing during the Vietnam War to locate underground tunnels dug by the Vietcong. Albert Einstein, who was also a dowser, wrote, "The dowsing rod is a simple instrument which shows the reaction of the human nervous system to certain factors which are unknown to us at this time."

If you've seen pictures of people dowsing, you probably noticed they used two rods, one in each hand. For instance, if someone was dowsing for water, they'd walk holding the rods in front of them. When the rods turned toward each other to form an "X" shape, that meant they were standing on a spot where they could successfully dig their well. But in fact, you don't need *two* rods in order to dowse for something. You can get the same result by holding one rod; when it turns, you know you've found what you've been looking for. So when you do a space clearing, you need only one dowsing rod, not two. This is convenient because it gives you one hand free to hold your pendulum, which you'll also use in space clearing.

Just like your pendulum, a dowsing rod is a simple tool; it has no magical or mystical powers! It's usually just an L-shaped metal rod as shown in the following image.

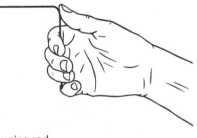

A dowsing rod

You can make a dowsing rod out of a metal clothes hanger or any bendable metal, such as a thin, 12-inch length of welding rod from a hardware store. You may want to start out with a simple homemade dowsing rod, so you can jump into learning right now. In the long run, however, just for ease of use, it's better to get one that's been deliberately made for dowsing. (I've listed Resources in the back of this book to help you.)

How to Hold Your Dowsing Rod

Just like with the pendulum, you need to learn how to use your dowsing rod. Here are some basic guidelines:

1. Hold it in a firm but relaxed fashion. Make sure you're not grasping it too tightly because when you use it, the rod will need to turn to point in different directions. If you're clenching it in a death grip, it won't be able to swing freely!

2. Place your thumb very lightly on the top of the rod, right at the place where the bend is. But don't press down hard with your thumb—again, that would prevent it from moving from side to side.

3. Hold the rod out in front of you just a bit, with your arm relaxed and slightly bent, just like you see in the following image.

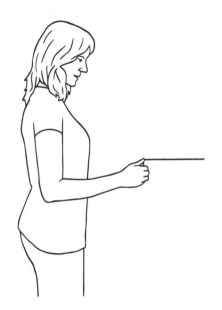

Using a dowsing rod

4. Always keep the dowsing rod pointing straight forward. You can think of it as if you're pointing a flashlight in front of you, trying to find your way in the dark.

5. Hold the rod parallel to the ground or else pointing just ever so slightly downward. If you point it up, it will tend to flop off to one side.

Now you'll learn how to use the rod to explore your environment. Just like the pendulum, the rod responds to the question you're holding in your mind. In other words, it needs to know what you're looking for. Practice by finding the flow of the energy in your house with the following two exercises.

Exercise: Discover If the Qi
Is Coming into Your House

In feng shui, the front door of your house is called "the mouth of qi." It's where the flow of nourishing energy enters your space to feed its life-force, just like your mouth is where food enters your body. If a space is in a healthy state, there will be a good flow of qi coming through the front door. But if there's stagnation or a buildup of stress held in the house, it can reduce or even block the qi from entering. So one early indicator of the health of a space is to use your dowsing rod to check if there is qi coming in your front door. Here's how to do it:

1. Stand inside your house to one side of the front door. (It doesn't have to be open.)

2. Hold the dowsing rod in front of you with the point facing forward.

3. Tell yourself, *I'm looking for the qi flowing in through the door.*

4. Walk slowly, parallel to the door, keeping that thought in mind.

5. As you pass by the doorway, you should see your rod begin to turn to point into the house. If so, you've located the energy flowing in!

Qi coming in the front door.

You can think of it as if there's a stream coming in through the front door, and as the rod came into contact with it, the current made it turn in the direction the water is flowing. (You can see a video demonstrating how to do this exercise at www.jeanhaner.com/clearingvideos.)

If you find qi coming into your home, that doesn't mean the space doesn't need clearing! But it *is* a sign that at least you're getting some nourishment from your environment.

If your rod doesn't turn but instead continues to point straight ahead as you pass by the front door, that means there is no qi coming in. This is usually an indication that there's so much stress or residue built up, it's blocking energy from coming in to support you in your home. In that case, you may even be using up some of your own personal qi to boost the vitality of the space—and this is not what we want! The space should be nourishing you rather than the other way around.

Exercise: Follow the Flow of Qi in Your Home

Even if your rod doesn't turn at the front door, it doesn't mean there's *no* qi in your house! There will still be some energy flowing in the space. So now you'll learn how to locate it.

1. Choose a room in your house and hold the dowsing rod out in front of you as you've just learned to do. Tell yourself, *I'm looking for the qi flow.* Start to walk very slowly through the room.

2. After a few steps, you may notice that the rod turns slightly. If it does, you should turn your body to follow it, positioning yourself so that the rod is still pointing forward, straight ahead of you. In other words, always keep the rod at a 90-degree angle to your body. If the rod starts to point to the left or right, move your body to follow, to keep the rod always pointing in front of you. (You can watch a brief video that shows you exactly how to move with the rod at www.jeanhaner.com/clearingvideos.)

3. If the rod curves off in a certain direction, what's happening is that it's showing you how the qi is moving through the space. Keep walking while you hold in mind, *I'm looking for the qi flow;* the rod should take you on a looping journey throughout the room!

When the qi flow is healthy, it moves in curves throughout the space, and it goes everywhere in the room. There should not be an area of the room where the rod doesn't end up taking you.

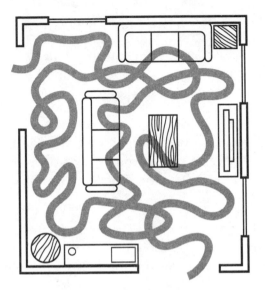

Healthy qi flow in a room.

Do this exercise a few times until it feels natural to you. Common mistakes are:

- *Walking too slowly.* If you're extremely slow or tentative, the rod won't be responsive. Relax and try a *slightly* faster speed of moving through the room.

- *Walking too fast.* If you move too quickly, the rod won't have a chance to turn. Slow down and keep your eyes on the rod; as you see it change direction, turn to follow.

- *Getting distracted.* If your mind wanders, you're no longer focused on the thought, *I'm looking for the qi flow.* If you start thinking about what to make for dinner, the rod will wander just like your thoughts. With dowsing, the secret to getting the right answer is asking the right question! In other words, keep your mind focused on what you're looking for and don't let your attention stray.

Just like with any new skill, it takes some practice before it becomes second nature. You'll be amazed at how quickly you won't have to concentrate so much, and the dowsing rod will feel like it's part of you!

Clearing Emotional Residue

If some emotional stress is held in the room, your dowsing rod won't take you in graceful curves around the space. Instead, when it locates a spot holding some stress, it'll usually turn in a tight spiral, meaning you'll also end up spiraling around as you follow it.

If this happens, congratulations! You've found your first area to clear. It's a place where the qi is no longer flowing in a healthy manner but instead has become disturbed. Perhaps it's where someone had a fright years ago, and the intensity of that emotion embedded itself there. Or maybe it's where you sit when you pay your bills and have unknowingly downloaded some worry into the environment repeatedly over time. But you can clear it and then the energy will flow freely again.

Here's how to clear emotional residue held in a room:

1. Use your dowsing rod to follow the qi flow in the room until the rod turns in a spiral. (You can see an example in a video at www.jeanhaner.com/clearingvideos.)

If you're curious about the origin of this disturbance, you can ask your pendulum, "Is this from previous occupants of this space?" If you get a "no," then ask, "Is this from one of the current occupants?" You can even ask what kind of emotion is held there, such as anger, fear, anxiety, etc. However, you don't have to get details about the cause; you can simply go ahead and clear it.

2. Stand on or near the spot, holding your pendulum. Check over your palm to make sure you're not switched. If your system is in balance, you can proceed.

3. Tell yourself you're going to clear the stress held in this one spot. And then, just like when you do a personal clearing for someone, your pendulum will start swinging.

4. While the pendulum is in motion, just hold the thought in mind that you're clearing this disturbance.

5. Stay aware of how you're feeling—just like when you're clearing a person, you might get some impressions that have to do with the energy that's being released. For example, if some anxiety is imprinted in the environment, then as it's clearing, you might feel anxious or start breathing more shallowly. You might even get an image in your mind's eye of what the person was stressed about. It's just your system "reading" the information as it clears. And *then* you may feel a gentle, barely perceptible little shift or even a big lovely *whoosh* as the clearing happens! But it's not a requirement to feel anything.

6. Trust your tools to guide you during the clearing. Your pendulum will let you know when the clearing is complete, just as it does when you're doing a personal clearing: its movement will change when it's done.

7. Once you've cleared that little area of stressed energy, turn your dowsing rod to face forward and start following

the qi flow again. Perhaps your rod will take you in curves throughout the rest of the room, but it's likely it'll soon locate another little spiral; then you'll know you've found a second bit of stress held in the room. If your dowsing rod doesn't move in a spiral but instead goes in a sharp zigzag motion or in a very straight line right across the room, these movements also indicate unhealthy qi flow. Stop, pick up your pendulum, and clear these spots just as you did the other one.

8. Continue following your rod until it completes its journey around the room and starts to head back out the door. But before you leave, make sure that you have indeed traveled to each part of the room and the rod hasn't avoided any major areas.

If the energy's stagnant in one corner of the room, for instance, the rod may not even take you there. You're telling the dowsing rod to follow the flow of qi, but if the qi is blocked from going into that part of the space, that means there's no flow to follow!

9. If you do find a substantial area of the room where the rod won't go, that means there's something there to clear. In this case, just change the question you're holding in your mind. Instead of saying, "Follow the flow of qi," tell your rod, "Take me to the disturbance that's blocking the qi in that area." The rod will then move you there and spiral you around when it's located the stressed spot, and you can clear it as usual.

It's really fun to use a dowsing rod as it leads you through the space and moves in different ways to let you know you've found some invisible energy that needs to be cleared!

The Primary Disturbance (PD)

The exercises you've just done with following the qi flow and clearing old emotions held in the space are good practice to help you develop your skills. When you do a full space clearing, however, there's an initial step before you follow the qi flow. In any environment, there's always one energetic imbalance that's stronger than all the rest. This is called the Primary Disturbance (PD).

The PD may be the spot where someone had a single traumatic experience decades ago. Or it may be the couch where you and your spouse have had repeated arguments over the years, each one adding to the layers of negativity until the disturbed energy develops quite a magnitude. It is often strong enough to keep some separate minor disturbances in place just through the power of its influence. So if you clear the Primary Disturbance first, it can affect the vibration of the entire space; then some of the minor disturbances that were held there just because of the PD will disappear, making the rest of the clearing go more quickly.

So after you've determined the ratio of yin to yang and learned whether the qi is coming in the front door, your next step is to locate the Primary Disturbance. In most cases, it's somewhere in the house. Once in a great while, it may actually be located on a neighboring property or even farther away but is transmitting a strong influence into your space. For example, one house I cleared had originally been the servants' quarters of a mansion down the street. The PD was actually located in the mansion because the servants' lives had been so entangled with their employers'. In another case, a neighbor was mentally ill and sending such negative intentions into my client's home that it severely disturbed the energy there.

How to Find the Primary Disturbance

Ask your pendulum, "Is the Primary Disturbance located on this property?"

If your pendulum says "yes": Ask your dowsing rod to take you there.

Point the rod forward and start to slowly walk, following the rod until it turns sharply or spins you in a spiral to indicate you've found the spot. The rod may take you on a bit of a wandering journey through the house because it's responding to your attempts to hold the thought in mind and home in on that energy. So don't be dismayed if you feel like you're on a wild goose chase! Just keep holding the thought in mind that you're looking for the PD and you'll get there.

If your pendulum says "no": The PD isn't on this property, and you can just clear it from where you stand.

You don't need to know the exact location of the PD or the source of a disturbance. Remember you don't have to be physically present with a person or a place to clear it. What matters is that the clearing happens; you don't have to turn into Sherlock Holmes.

However, in this situation, you may *want* to determine the general location of the PD because that can help you understand what it is. One option is to point your finger in different directions and ask till you get a "yes" and then clear the PD from where you are. As usual, stay aware of what you're feeling, as that can help you recognize what the disturbance relates to.

So you could point to the north and ask your pendulum, "Is the PD in this direction?" If you get a "yes" and you realize you're pointing toward the house of a troubled neighbor or the high school down the street, that can help you make sense of things. You could also use your pendulum to ask, "Is this to do with the neighbor/high school?"

After clearing the PD, return to the front door to check the qi flow again.

If qi wasn't coming in the front door when you first checked, it's possible that just clearing the PD released enough of the block so that the qi can now enter. You may find your rod turns to point into the house, to indicate the energy's now coming in.

Alternatively, you may be shocked to see the rod turn to point *out* the front door! Don't worry, nothing's gone wrong. This happens sometimes as a sign that disturbed energy is streaming out of the house; it's a good sign.

Continuing the Clearing

Once you have released the PD, you can start dowsing for emotional residue throughout the house, room by room. Begin with whatever room you enter into from the front door, and then once you're finished, let the rod decide where to go afterward. It may take you into the room right next to it, or it might lead you elsewhere in the house. Trust the way the dowsing rod is following how the energy moves in the space.

In some rooms, there will be just a few places where your rod will spin to let you know some disturbed energy is stuck there. In other spaces, you may find that you have to stop to clear every few steps! It's rare to dowse a room where your rod doesn't find any disturbances at all.

Most of what you'll find to clear are the accumulated layers of thoughts and feelings that have been repeated there daily for years, like the stress held in your desk chair from all the times you've worked at your computer or the daily worries of a previous occupant as they cooked dinner at the stove. Occasionally, you'll clear an area where a single intense experience was powerful enough to lock the emotion there. For instance, if there was an accident, an act of violence, or a traumatic shock, that event could be imprinted in that spot, even though it happened only once.

No matter why the stressed energy is held in a space, you clear it in the same way: Let your pendulum go into its clearing movement, and pay attention to what you feel as you clear. At first, you'll probably feel no different when you tune in to an area of emotional residue, but after some practice and experience, you may well start to get feelings or impressions, just like when you clear a person.

How to Share Your Impressions

If you're doing space clearing for a friend, it can be interesting for them to hear about impressions you get while you're clearing because they may be able to understand why you're feeling that way. It can be helpful for you to hear their explanation as well. For example, at one house, my rod spun in a large open corner of the master bedroom. As I cleared, the energy felt thick and heavy—and then, oddly, sweaty and dirty! I made a joke as I shared this with my client, and she laughed and said, "You have no idea how right you are! That's where my husband and I dump our dirty clothes every night. I just cleaned it up because you were coming today."

In some cases, you may feel embarrassed to share an impression because it seems too vague or weird. Sometimes, you'll be sure that you must be imagining things. I remember the very first time some clients paid for my airfare and hotel expenses to do space clearings. Peter and Marie were a married couple who hired me to clear the energy of several East Coast properties that they owned. I was so excited to work with them but also nervous that they'd end up regretting paying so much extra for all my travel expenses. So on my first day, as the two of them accompanied me to clear their family home, I had some performance anxiety.

My nervousness only increased when my dowsing rod spun wildly by a rocking chair in their master bedroom and the distinct image burst into my mind of a pair of gigantic, bright red lips floating in midair! Furthermore, these lips were pursed in an expression of extreme disapproval and contempt. *What in the world might this mean?* I wondered.

I desperately tried to download some more information so I wouldn't sound like a total idiot if I shared this with my clients. But nothing more came through, and I was so embarrassed, I couldn't even look at them as I mumbled, "Well, this is going to sound really silly, but I keep seeing a huge pair of lips, painted bright red, and they seem to be expressing some displeasure . . . Um . . . Do you know anything about the history of this rocking chair?"

There was total silence in response. My anxiety got worse! I started having fantasies about being unceremoniously taken back to the airport and put on the first plane out of town. Then I heard a deep gasp, and Marie shouted, "Oh my *god*, it's your mother!"

As it turned out, Peter's mother had been famous within the community for wearing fire-engine-red lipstick as well as constantly holding her mouth pursed in a very contorted way. This negative, unhappy woman had disapproved of their marriage. She'd hated Marie and made sure everyone knew about it till the day she died. Of course, this was her rocking chair and her ghost was actually sitting in that chair. Her attachment to her son and hatred of his wife had kept her from passing on.

Marie said, "I *knew* it! We both can feel her every night, rocking in that chair, glaring at us in bed! Can you *please* clear her?"

As I stood there clearing, I felt the mother's resistance and anger gradually start to transform. Then suddenly, in what felt like a bubble popping, her presence disappeared in an instant. I turned to look at Peter and Marie, and their mouths were hanging open. They'd felt it too.

If I'd allowed my fear of looking stupid to stop me from sharing what I was seeing, I would not have had this confidence-boosting experience, and Peter and Marie would have been deprived of the confirmation that what they'd been feeling was not just in their imagination. So if an emotion, sensation, or impression comes to you when you're doing a space clearing, try not to worry about how silly or inconsequential it may seem. Just like in a personal clearing, share the raw information without trying to interpret it, and you might be surprised at what you find out!

Ghosts

You may feel nervous at the thought of finding a ghost in a space! It can bring up all kinds of scary ideas about spirits intending you harm. So let's have a talk about what a ghost really is.

First of all, there's a range to the kind of energies that can get stuck in a space from someone who used to live there, but most of them have nothing to do with a ghost.

There is the usual emotional residue, which is what the dowsing rod finds when you follow the qi flow. There can even be what's like a "memory imprint" from someone who lived in the space over many years. If you're sensitive, this can be something you distinctly sense as you do a clearing. But you'll still find it even if you don't feel anything. Your rod will spin when it comes across this imprint because it's like the other psychic house dust that's interfering with the qi flow. It can feel like a stronger disturbance than the others, and you may even wonder if it's a ghost—but it's not.

For instance, I once cleared a house where the previous owner had been a piano teacher. For 30 years, she'd given lessons in her living room, sitting on that piano bench day after day, doing the same thing over and over. When I reached the part of the room where the piano had been, it was almost like a movie running in that spot. I could see her and feel how her repeated thoughts and behavior had engraved themselves in the space. But *she* wasn't there, just the deep imprint of her energy.

A ghost is different. A ghost is someone's spirit that is stuck in the space. Their body died, but their spirit didn't successfully pass over; this can happen for a variety of reasons. They may be so attached to the place or the people they care about that they can't leave as they should. They may be confused and not even realize they're dead because they died so suddenly and don't understand what happened.

No matter the reason, when someone's spirit is caught here, they need help to get free, to pass over. It's never right that someone can't move on after death; their time on earth is over and they're not meant to stay here. Clearing can help liberate them to move on and complete their soul's journey.

If you encounter a ghost when you're space-clearing, what will usually happen is that the ghost will run away from you. They're confused and probably frightened, and when they see you, all bright and shiny, dangling your pendulum and waving your dowsing rod around, that can scare them! So, especially in the early stages of learning to clear, you likely won't come across a ghost, even if there is one. They'll hide from you, or go for a walk around the block till you're gone!

And if you're afraid to discover a ghost because you don't feel prepared to deal with it, rest assured that you won't even find one. With clearing, you will find only disturbances that you are *able* to clear. The rest will be beyond your awareness.

Know that, just because there's been a death in a house, that doesn't mean there's a ghost there or that the house will have a high level of disturbed energy. Death is a natural part of life, and many homes have been lived in by people who passed away there after a long, happy life. So you don't have to be afraid of clearing a house where someone has died; it doesn't mean you'll encounter unusual problems. If anything, you'll clear any suffering they endured or the grief of the people they left behind. It can be a very sacred experience to clear a house after a death.

How to Clear a Ghost

To clear a ghost, you don't chase it around the place with your dowsing rod, yelling, "Wait, I can help you!" Once you're experienced with this work and can easily stay in clearing mode, what will usually happen is that, after the ghost has a chance to check you out, it'll come to *you*. In other words, it will sense the soft and mindful way of being that you're holding as you work, and it will start to trust you, feel safer, and then be drawn to you. When you clear a ghost, you often do experience a profoundly beautiful sensation as they pass. Once you've cleared a ghost, you'll hope to do it again soon!

For example, once I took a group of advanced students on a field trip to practice space clearing in an old Victorian hotel. What they didn't know is that 80 years before, an old woman named Agnes was murdered there, and the employees believed she had haunted the place ever since. They said Agnes played tricks on them, locking cleaning staff in the rooms and making noises to frighten guests.

Several of the students discovered Agnes with their dowsing rods but by the time they pulled out their pendulums to clear her, she was gone, having run away to hide again. Finally, we gathered as a group in a hallway, and I explained that all we needed to do was take out our pendulums and just go into clearing mode.

After a few minutes, at the far end of the hall, I saw a faint image of Agnes; she semi-materialized and stood there, watching us. As we maintained that openhearted state, she drew closer and closer until she was standing right next to me. Then I felt her slowly start to relax; I heard her take a deep, slow breath and she faded away. In the next moment a huge wave of what felt like joy and gratitude swept over all of us as she seemed to say her thanks and good-bye.

❀

As you've followed the qi flow and cleared emotional stress held in the space, you've already deeply transformed the vibrations of your home. But there are other ways that the energy in your environment can need clearing. Next, we'll look at how the earth underneath your feet may need some loving kindness too!

Chapter 9

How to Clear
Geopathic Stress

The energy of the earth beneath your home can also affect your experience there. The earth has natural meridians of energy running through it just like your body does, and if these become stressed, they can radiate that disturbed information up into your space. This can affect everything from the quality of your sleep to your ability to focus at your desk—and even your overall sense of well-being.

When the energy of the earth is out of balance, it's called geopathic stress (GS). "Geo" means earth and "pathic" means suffering, so this term conveys that the earth is suffering. And often the suffering of the earth is caused by the people living on it! For example, when a new shopping center or subdivision is built, they dig into the earth, cutting into the lines of energy that naturally run there. Slicing through the ground can alter the flow of life-force there; then, instead of healthy qi moving in the land, the qi becomes out of balance. This can affect the energy throughout the neighborhood, broadcasting stress horizontally along the lines as well as upward, possibly into your home or business.

I was once brought in to do a space clearing for a business that had been experiencing problems ever since moving into new headquarters. Their large suite of offices had originally belonged to a company that had gone bankrupt. They'd even purchased all the furniture of the failed business, thrilled that they'd gotten such a deal. Will, the CEO, said to me, "I especially hope you can clear this one office that everyone calls the 'Room of Doom.' Of the eight people who've worked there since we moved in, seven have been fired and the eighth moved to a new office after two weeks."

I expected to find a very high percentage of yin energy in the space because of all the emotional stress felt there. I smugly assumed the cause of their problems was obviously due to what had been imprinted by previous occupants. In other words, the residue of all the stress felt by the employees of the former company as everything fell apart was not only stuck in the space but infused in all the furniture they'd left behind as well! And the Room of Doom? Well, of course, each of those employees who used that office would have been affected by the leftover feelings of the previous ones, and layered their own negative experience on top, increasing the chance that the next occupant would fail as well.

I got a surprise when my pendulum measured the energy in the office suite to be 20 percent yin, 80 percent yang! There could be only two reasons for this. Either there'd been a lot of intense anger experienced there—or the earth energies were out of balance. (Earth energies are mostly yang.)

When I asked my dowsing rod to lead me to the Primary Disturbance in the place, it took me to an attractive office with big windows overlooking the greenery outside. Will was immediately impressed. "Ah, you found it!" he said, laughing. "This is the Room of Doom." As I used the rod to explore the energy, I discovered the geopathic stress in the room was massive.

I asked Will if he knew of any recent construction in the neighborhood. He said, "No, not in the neighborhood, but I understand that about two years before we moved in, they did a huge project right here, digging under the existing building to create an underground parking garage. In fact, you're standing over the entrance." I peered out the window, and sure enough, the driveway into the garage was directly beneath this "doomed" office.

What had happened was that the excavation had created severe stress in the earth, which was also being transmitted up into the offices above. Geopathic stress can be broadcast several stories up; you don't have to be on the ground floor to be affected by it. The downturn for the previous business had started soon after the work on the garage had begun, so it was possible that the GS could have been at least a factor in its eventual bankruptcy.

The Earth Has Its Own Needs

The earth has natural needs to release certain forms of energy in order to maintain harmony; that's not a problem. However, it can become a problem for *us* when we show up and plop our house down on one of these areas. This is because, depending on what's being released in that spot, the energy can affect the human system in detrimental ways. When we find a spot where the earth's energy may stress our own, this also falls into the general category of GS; even though the earth may not be out of balance, the information being released is not beneficial for people to live near.

In some parts of the world, before a house is constructed, a dowser is brought in to evaluate the energy of the earth and advise on the best place on the property for the house to be built. Imagine if development everywhere could be done with such conscious care! At least with clearing, we have the power to discover if the earth energies where you live are stressful for your system. Then we can clear the adverse affects, so you can live peacefully on your land.

There are three main sources of geopathic stress: magnetic fields, faulting pressure, and underground water.

Magnetic Fields

The earth has a magnetic field, as do our own bodies. However, there are natural fluctuations or distortions in the earth's magnetic field that can stress the human system. Along with these naturally occurring disturbances in the geomagnetic field, stress there can be created by people cutting into the earth, such as when a road or house is built, or utility pipes or wires are installed underground. That stress can be carried in the land for some distance, to affect you in your space.

A disturbance in a magnetic field can make you feel mildly unwell every time you're near it. It can interfere with your ability to concentrate if one runs in the land under your desk, or prevent restful sleep if it's beneath your bed. One woman who found that a stressed magnetic field ran under one side of her bed realized that was probably why she never slept on that side—and not even her dog would sleep there!

Dogs, like most animals, naturally sense and avoid disturbing earth energies. However, some animals, such as cats, are attracted to them. If your cat always sleeps in the same place, and it's not the warmest spot in the house, you might find some GS there! Rodents, wasps, ants, and many other types of insects are also attracted to GS; so if you have an infestation, it might be a symptom of GS on your property.

Just as the energy of the earth affects us, we affect it as well! Your difficult experience in a space can be transmitted into the earth and change its condition, just as a change in the earth can affect how *you* feel.

For instance, Katy, a 20-something interior designer, told me that she'd developed problems sleeping about nine months before. She'd feel fine until she went to bed, but then as she lay there, she'd start to feel sad and depressed and found it difficult to get to sleep. When she woke in the morning, she'd feel weak and listless, not her usual self.

When I used my dowsing rod to explore the room, I was astonished to discover line after line of stressed magnetic fields running through her entire bed. This was extremely unusual! Normally, you might find one or two lines, if any, in a room, spaced far apart. But these were packed tightly together, and they ran only under her bed; nowhere else in the room.

As I cleared them, Katy commented that the condo next to hers was vacant because her neighbor had just passed away. The woman had spent the last year in bed, dying of cancer. Katy said she often thought of her as she lay in bed because she knew her neighbor's pillow was directly behind her, on the other side of the common wall. And there was the likely explanation for the weird

phenomenon: her neighbor's suffering had been transmitted into the earth, and the disturbed magnetic fields
that formed under the neighbor's bed continued on to run
under Katy's bed as well.

Emotional trauma that happened in a particular spot
can change the energy of the land. It can be due to deep
emotions felt repeatedly over a period of time, as in the
dying neighbor, or from one traumatic experience, like an
act of violence.

Faulting Pressure

There are areas of naturally occurring pressure and
minor fracturing everywhere in the ground. This is not a
problem unless this pressure broadcasts energy into your
living space in a way that adversely affects you. In addition, human interference can cause problems; for example, the practice of fracking, which does damage to the
earth in the search to access natural gas.

When you're doing a space clearing, hold in mind that
you're looking for "faulting pressure." (We use this as a
generic term for any pressure or fracturing in the earth
that's negatively affecting your system.) If your pendulum indicates that there is faulting pressure affecting your
home, it doesn't mean that there are actual fault lines running underneath you or that the physical integrity of the
structure of your home is at risk. It just means you're being
subtly affected by this influence from the earth.

If there's faulting pressure in the land under your dining room table, for instance, it can make everyone feel
uncomfortable just below their conscious awareness. The
result can be that, even if you arrive at the table happy to
be together and the meal is delicious, dinner turns into

arguments or indigestion or both. People can't understand why they were in a perfectly good mood beforehand, but soon they're feeling irritated or food just isn't sitting well in their stomach.

Underground Water

Just like magnetic fields and faulting pressure, there is naturally occurring underground water everywhere—and that's a good thing! That is, unless it's transmitting stressed information up into your home.

The energy in underground water can become disturbed in a number of ways. First, as water flows through underground passages, it produces its own electromagnetic field, which can become distorted depending on how it's moving and the speed it's going, or if it crosses another underground stream or runs along a stressed magnetic field or area of faulting pressure as it flows. Any of these factors can cause it to stress the humans living above it. It can even create natural gamma or microwave radiation, which are not good for people at all.

Then you also must consider any stressful information the water might be carrying. If high levels of toxins are dissolved in it, they can be sending subtle vibrations of toxicity up into the house. And if, for example, the water flowed under a prison miles away before arriving beneath your house, it could also have soaked in disturbed energy from the people in the prison, and *that* energy could be circulating up into your space as well.

If there's disturbed water energy beneath you, you might feel mildly dizzy or slightly nauseated at times, or get hot and sweaty and toss off the blankets as you sleep. It can certainly contribute to an overall feeling of discomfort, emotionally or physically; but just like most GS, the influence is so subtle that until you learn it's there and connect the dots, you probably never think, *Huh, I always feel yucky in this part of the house.*

Everyone has their own unique sensitivity to earth energies. Some people are extremely affected by magnetic fields and others by underground water or faulting pressure; but GS is always a subtle background stressor even for the hardiest of people. You may be astonished to discover, once you learn to tune in, how different you feel when you're standing on an area of disturbed earth energy.

Clearing Geopathic Stress

So let's explore a room in your house now, and clear the adverse effects of any stressed earth energies there. Looking for GS is different from looking for emotional disturbances held in the space. Instead of taking your dowsing rod and concentrating on following the qi flow, you first take out your pendulum and ask a few questions.

1. Ask: "Is there any geopathic stress in this room?"
Not all rooms will be affected by GS. If you get a "no," try another room or area of your house until you get a "yes."

2. When you get a "yes," the next step is to find out which of the three types of GS there are in this space.
It's possible to have all three kinds of GS in a room, but you'll be clearing each kind one by one. Ask each of the following questions separately, and note whether you get a "yes" or "no" for each one:

- "Are there any disturbed magnetic fields?"
- "Is there any faulting pressure?"
- "Is there any stressed underground water?"

These three questions are actually the short versions of what we really mean when we ask about GS. As you're first learning, it can help to start out by asking the longer version of each question, listed below:

- "Are there any disturbed magnetic fields in this room that are adversely affecting the people who live here?"
- "Is there faulting pressure in this room that is adversely affecting the people who live here?"
- "Is there any naturally occurring underground water here that is adversely affecting the people who live here?" (You have to hold in mind that you're looking for "naturally occurring underground water"— otherwise, your dowsing rod might locate all the plumbing in the house!)

Do you see the difference between the short and long versions of the question? Because we each have different sensitivities to earth energies, if you ask only whether there's a "disturbed magnetic field," for example, you might unconsciously tune into one that would bother you—but it might not be one that your friend would be sensitive to. If you're doing a space clearing for a friend, when you look for GS in their house, you need to look for GS that is adversely affecting your *friend*, not you. Since this is their house, you need to be dowsing and clearing for their well-being there, not yours!

It is so important to hold a focused thought in mind when you're dowsing because if you're not asking the right question, you won't get the right answer! Once you have some experience, your system will have been trained to automatically know what you mean when you ask the shorter questions, but you get to that point by first using the longer versions.

3. Once you know what kinds of GS are in a room, you need to locate them.

Let's say you got a "yes" when you asked your pendulum if there were any disturbed magnetic fields. Take your dowsing rod and walk slowly in a straight line across the width of the room, telling yourself that you're looking for a disturbed magnetic field.

4. If your rod turns as you walk, then pause and either remember that spot or place a marker there so you can find it again.

If there is a field running across the room, then as you reach that spot, your rod will turn. You can imagine the field like an invisible wall of energy rising up from the floor, and when your rod encounters it, it'll be as if bumping into the wall makes it turn.

5. Straighten your rod so it faces forward again, and continue dowsing till you reach the opposite wall.

You may or may not find more stressed magnetic fields; if you do, be sure to note each one.

6. Then walk slowly across the *length* of the room in the same way.

This will allow you to find any stressed magnetic fields that may be running in the other direction. Mark any places the rod turns here as well.

You have now mapped out where stressed magnetic fields are affecting you in this room. You may not discover very many; it's common to find only one or two.

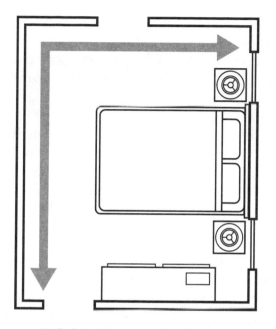

Walk the width and length of the room
to find lines of geopathic stress.

7. Stand on one of the spots where your rod turned to indicate a disturbed field. Take a moment to tune in and see how you feel.

You normally wouldn't be aware of feeling anything, but now that you're getting used to accessing information in a different way, don't be surprised if you feel a sensation in your body or just notice that something seems a bit off.

It's valuable to practice sensing the energy in this way because it's likely that you'll get the same feeling every time in the future that you encounter a disturbed magnetic field (or whatever GS you're dowsing for). Pretty soon, you'll need only a dowsing rod to confirm your findings because your body will have already told you something's there!

8. Now you must find out if the field can be cleared. Ask your pendulum, "Can this disturbance be cleared?"

When you were clearing old emotions held in the space, you didn't need to ask if they could be cleared; you just cleared them. But this is a different situation. Sometimes the earth needs to emit a certain vibration in a spot and it's not possible to clear its influence. This rarely happens, but if you don't check, you could be standing there trying to clear it, your pendulum swinging and swinging, while you're wondering what's taking so long!

If you get a "yes":

Then go ahead and clear it just like you'd clear any other stress. Pay attention to how you feel as the clearing happens and you may notice the energy shift! Earth energy is stronger than most other kinds, so it's a good opportunity to practice your sensing skills. If you're very sensitive, however, you might not want to stand directly on the magnetic line, but instead stand back a few feet. This isn't because there's any danger, but just because it might be too intense for you to be comfortable feeling it. You don't have to be physically in contact with the field for the clearing to be effective.

If you get a "no":

Very rarely, you'll get a "no," indicating that this field can't be cleared because the earth needs it to be there. In that case, you have a couple of choices. If the line of energy doesn't run under an important place in the house, you can just let it stay there. If it's not in a place where you spend a lot of time, like your bed, desk, or couch, then it's not affecting you very often and there's little concern. In that case, you can just let it be.

But if this line does run under your bed, for example, we don't want it stressing you each night as you sleep. In a situation like this, you can make a friendly request of the earth, asking if it would be so kind as to move the field just a few feet away so it's no longer affecting you in the same way. You ask your pendulum, "Can this field be moved away from the bed?"

If you get a "yes," just start clearing as usual, and the pendulum will indicate when it's complete. (In cases like these, I almost always get a "yes.") Usually, the line moves enough of a distance from its original position; for instance, to an outside wall or into the closet, so that it's no longer in a troublesome place. If you'd like, you can use the dowsing rod to check its new position.

If, however, you get a "no," that this line of energy cannot be shifted, then you might want to consider moving your bed so the field is no longer beneath you as you sleep. Again, it's highly unusual for this situation to occur. Almost always, fields can be cleared or moved.

9. If you found more than one stressed magnetic line in the room, go ahead and clear the rest, one by one, in the same way.

Never try to clear more than one at a time; earth energy is very powerful, and it'd be too demanding on your system to tune in to more than one at a time.

10. If your pendulum told you there was also underground water and/or faulting pressure that was adversely affecting you in this room, repeat the same process for the other forms of GS.

Here's some good news: You only have to look for GS on the main floor of your house. You don't have to search for it on the upper floors because if you've cleared it on the main floor, it's no longer radiating up into the house. Stress is being broadcast from the earth under the building, so once it's cleared on the lower level, it's no longer affecting the space.

If you have a basement, you might think that you should clear GS there instead of the main floor. However, in many cases, the footprint of the basement is not as large as the floor above it, so if you dowse there, you could miss areas of GS that are affecting the living area above. On that same note, if a floor above the main one extends beyond its footprint, you should dowse for GS in those areas.

Pace Yourself

When we open up to the energy of the earth, it's different from connecting to the energy of a person or some human emotions left in a space. People hold back; they'll release only a little at a time. The intensity of an emotion stuck in a room is nowhere near as powerful as GS—the earth does not hold back!

So when you're working consciously with earth energies, you're working with stronger information. It can be more tiring than working with people's energies. Do *not* disregard the instruction to clear only one line of GS at a time. If you try to clear all the GS in a room all at once, you're going to end up exhausted, or the clearing won't be complete. Be sure to frequently check to see if you're switched, and if the pendulum does indicate this, believe it.

And remember to pace yourself! Listen to your body. If you're starting to feel tired, then take a break, drink some water, have a meal or a rest, and then come back later. You need to allow yourself time to build your muscles with this work. It doesn't matter if you stop halfway through the space clearing—the house's energy won't be lopsided! You've brought back some balance, and things are correspondingly better.

You now know how to locate and clear emotional stress and imbalanced earth energies in any environment, but there's one more important factor in clearing a space. Next we'll see how you can avoid being stressed by the invisible effects of modern technology.

chapter 10

How to Clear Adverse Effects of Technology

Keith couldn't figure it out. He'd always been the family cook and looked forward to coming home at the end of the day to make dinner. But ever since they'd moved to their new house, he didn't even want to go in the kitchen. More and more, he was just stopping to get takeout on the way home, and everyone was complaining that they missed his cooking.

Keith explained all this to me as I cleared their house, and when I arrived at the kitchen, I said, "Let's try an experiment." I stepped far back into the dining room and, holding my dowsing rod, I said, "Show me how close Keith can get to the stove before he's adversely affected by its electromagnetic field." I slowly walked toward the kitchen, and the moment I stepped in the doorway, the rod turned.

In their previous house, the stove had been gas, which didn't use anywhere near the same amount of current as this electric one in their new house. And from 10 feet away, Keith's system began to be stressed by its electromagnetic field (EMF). On an unconscious level, his body told him it didn't feel good near the stove, and this was why he had an aversion to even going into the kitchen. His arms weren't long enough to cook there without feeling uncomfortable!

Everyone has a different sensitivity to EMFs. When I did the same experiment to see how close Hannah, Keith's wife, could get to the stove, I could walk right up to it. But that didn't mean Hannah had to take on the job of chief cook! Just like the other kinds of energy in the house, adverse effects of EMFs can be cleared. And a few days after the space clearing, I got an e-mail from Hannah: "The world is right again—we're back to my husband's home-cooked dinners!"

The Adverse Effects of Technology

In a space clearing, the third kind of energy you work with is the invisible energy of technology. We have all this wonderful technology that makes life easy and enjoyable: appliances, TVs, computers, cell phones, and an ever-increasing number of fun devices. And that's a good thing; it shows we're evolving and improving our lives in many ways. But you could say the human body is evolving at a different rate, and it's not able to adapt so quickly to some of the effects of technology.

All these various contraptions that use electrical current emit some degree of EMFs. Others, such as microwave ovens and cell phones, also emit microwave radiation. These stress the human system in varying ways and because we're surrounded by so many all day long, we're all dealing with a constant background stress.

There have been many studies about how these things affect us, with results that can be scary or reassuring. Some research says our health can be affected by cell phone use, for instance, while others say it's not a problem at all. I wonder if the news we get depends on the organization funding the study!

Everyone has a different level of sensitivity to technology. Some people are not very impacted. For others, the effects can be so disabling they have to seek refuge by trying to live off the grid. However, no matter what your sensitivity, you're now empowered to do something about it: you can clear. For example, you can discover if the EMF from your hair dryer is stressing your system every morning as you use it, and then you can clear that negative influence. This doesn't mean the EMF will no longer be there! Rather, that it'll no longer affect you in the same way.

So as you do a space clearing in every room, also ask if there are any adverse effects of technology on the people living there. If you get a "yes," then point to each device and ask if it needs to be cleared. If "yes," clear it, and your pendulum will indicate when the clearing is complete.

As you clear the negative influence of technology in the space, you might also ask your pendulum if your home's wireless system or the smart meter on the exterior wall of your home is disturbing your energy. As I said, we each have different levels of sensitivity to these kinds of things. You may not be adversely affected at all, but it's good to check.

Let's practice one aspect of this type of clearing now.

Exercise: Practice Clearing EMFs

Here's what to do to clear the adverse effects of electromagnetic fields:

1. Choose a room in the house where there's something that plugs in.

While you're still learning, I'd recommend not starting in the kitchen, as there are probably so many appliances there that your mind can get distracted by all the various sources of EMFs. Perhaps start in your bedroom, where there might be only a few things, such as a TV, table lamp, or cell phone charger.

2. Ask your pendulum, "Are there any electromagnetic fields in this room that are adversely affecting the people who live here?"

3. If you get a "yes," point at one of the objects and ask, "Does its EMF need to be cleared?"

4. If you get a "yes," then go into clearing mode as usual.

You can hold in mind that you're clearing the disturbing effects of the EMF from this appliance. It might help to visualize the disturbing field shrinking back into the device until it's contained inside. The pendulum will indicate when you're done.

5. Be sure to clear one device at a time.

If you stand in the room and try to clear everything there at once, it can be overwhelming for you. One of the most difficult things about clearing is learning to respect what a powerful experience it is to open to and work with the invisible energy around you. Don't take shortcuts!

Clearing the Adverse Effects of Microwave Radiation

Besides EMFs, it's good to check for microwave radiation from your microwave oven or cell phone. The process is exactly the same; you just slightly alter the question. For instance, in the kitchen, point at the microwave oven and ask, "Does its microwave radiation need to be cleared of the adverse effects on the people who use it?" With your own cell phone, ask, "Am I being adversely affected by the radiation from this phone?" (For someone else's cell phone, remember to ask if *they* are being adversely affected, not you.) If you get a "yes," then clear.

For things you use frequently, such as your computer or cell phone, it can be an interesting exercise to first test how much they're affecting you before you clear them, just as I did for Keith and the stove. For example:

- Take your dowsing rod and stand some distance away from your computer. Give yourself plenty of space; you might even want to stand in the next room.

- Tell your rod to indicate when it reaches the point where the computer's EMF starts stressing you.

- Walk slowly toward the computer; when the rod turns, you know that beyond that line you'll be adversely affected. You may be surprised at how far away that is!

It's amazing how powerful clearing can be here. In one clearing workshop, a chiropractor listened to his voice mail before he practiced clearing his cell phone. There were seven frantic messages from patients asking for the earliest possible appointment as they were in such pain.

Then he participated in the exercise of clearing his phone. When he got home later that evening and finally picked up his phone to return his patients' calls, he was astonished to find seven new voice mails from these people. They all said that things had changed; their pain was gone, so they could wait till their next scheduled appointment! Clearing the phone may have also extended out through the ethers to clear his patients as well.

There's No Need to Spend Money on Products

Over the past several years, various products have come on the market that claim to block the detrimental influences of computers, cell phones, etc. For instance, sometimes it's a crystal you're supposed to hang around your neck, or a little object you stick to your phone. What I've found is that the effectiveness of these things is extremely limited, as it depends on the level of consciousness of the person who *made* the device. If they're highly evolved and aware, then some of that energy has been inserted into the device and will benefit you for a certain amount of time and then wear off. I find that most of these things have a minor effect for a little while and then are useless.

What concerns me more is that I usually find that the person who made the device is not so conscious and aware! Instead, along with their sincerely good intentions, infused in this little object is also a thick gob of their energy, so it's broadcasting some of their personal drama to you every time you wear it or hold it close to you. So instead of being shielded from disturbing effects of EMFs, you're actually being subjected to the disturbing effects of their personality radiating from the product!

Special objects that supposedly protect you or fix a problem come from a very superficial understanding of energy. For one thing, it never works to try to be a technician, tinkering to force a desired change with some external contraption. This narrow outlook is also based on a fear-based judgment that you have to "protect" yourself from something "bad." This is a very simplistic view that doesn't recognize there is no bad or good energy; it's how we react to it that matters.

When you clear the adverse effects of a device, for instance, it actually transforms how your system reacts to the EMFs. This recognizes and respects the complex interrelationships among all things. When you clear the disturbing effects of anything in your environment, you're simultaneously training your system to stay in balance no matter what energy you encounter. Then there's no need to purchase products to "protect" you!

Trust and Respect the Power of This Work

Especially while you're first learning, pace yourself and don't push forward if you get tired. Check frequently to see if you're switched, and trust what your pendulum tells you. Your energetic system is learning a new way of being, and you need to allow yourself time to develop your abilities.

Watch out for how your desire to help can make you try too hard or take on too much. If you're reading this book, we already know you're a kind person who wants to make this world a better place! But your drive to help can make you disregard the protocol and end up causing you problems.

Teresa came to a clearing retreat and was inspired when she learned how to clear her cell phone. *Think of all the people in the world who don't know they're being stressed by their cell phones,* she mused. *I should help ease their suffering!* So she decided to clear all the cell phones in the world—all at once. She immediately got sick and spent the rest of the retreat in bed.

Just because you can't see anything visibly going on when you're clearing doesn't mean something powerful isn't happening. When Teresa opened up to clear *all* the cell phones in the world, it was too much for her. I can't emphasize enough that you have to respect the power and trust the process of this work.

chapter 11

Final Stages
of the Space Clearing

A s you complete the space clearing, don't forget the hallways, stairs, bathrooms, and the basement; any areas you spend time in. You don't need to climb into the closets, however! The clearing you do in the rooms will include what's in the closets. If something stored in a closet holds disturbed energy, your rod will spin right outside the closet door. If you're curious, you can ask your pendulum where the imbalance is: whether it's held in the spot you're standing, or if it's something inside the closet next to you that has stressed energy.

Furniture and objects on display can also transmit energy, of course, so if your dowsing rod indicates stress in a certain spot in the room, it could be that a chair or a memento on the shelf next to you is emanating information that's bothersome. I once cleared a psychiatrist's home and my dowsing rod spun next to each of three oil paintings in his den. "Those were done by a psychotic patient of mine as a thank-you for his treatment," he said. "I've never liked them, but I felt obligated to display them." *Yikes!* The artwork was radiating out disturbed energy imprinted by his patient as he created them. I'd have preferred that my client just take them down, since he didn't like them, but at least after the clearing their energy was no longer adversely affecting him!

Most garages don't require much attention because you probably don't spend time there, but if personal possessions are stored there that hold energy from your past, it's likely your dowsing rod will lead you there to clear them. If your garage has living space above it, check for GS there because it'll probably be radiating into that upper floor.

Is the Energy in a Clear and Balanced State?

After you've gone through every area of the house and cleared emotional residue, geopathic stress, and the adverse effects of technology—congratulations! Take a nice deep breath and have a seat! Then ask your pendulum, "Is the energy in this space in a clear and balanced state?" If "yes," hooray, you can move on to the final stages described on the following pages.

You'll almost always get a "yes" to that question. But if you get a "no," don't worry. It just means that somewhere in the house there's a little bit more to clear. It's not unusual to have this happen while you're still learning this work. You can then ask your pendulum, "Is there still something to clear on the main floor?" If you get a "no," then ask about the other floors till you get a "yes."

As you keep your mind focused on the thought that you're looking for the energy that still needs clearing, use your dowsing rod to find it, being aware that it may take you there on a bit of a wandering route. The rod will turn sharply or spin you in a spiral when you reach the spot. Ask if it's due to emotional residue or GS or technology; then clear it.

Once you're done, ask again with the pendulum, "Is this space in a clear and balanced state?" If you still get a "no," just repeat the same process again until you get a "yes" to that question. It's important to phrase the question this way rather than as "Am I done yet?" or "Is there anything more to clear?" because it's too easy to get lost in doubting yourself, overthinking, and going back to check and recheck. And when that happens, it's less and less likely you'll get accurate answers from your dowsing tools. So just ask that one simple question and you'll be able to stay on track.

Personal Clearings

Your space is now filling with a new vibrant energy, the qi flowing beautifully to provide the most nourishing and harmonious environment for your personal life journey! However, we can't ignore the fact that you and everyone living in the space are used to the old vibration. Yes, you sincerely want change, but what happens for all of us is that we get accustomed to the energy of our home. Even though we know there's stagnation or imbalance, it's our comfort zone. It's what we know, and although we want things to be different, our systems can unconsciously resist the new quality of energy. So unless we're brought into coherence with the new frequency of the space, we can bring it back down to the old comfort zone, even within days of the space clearing.

So, after a space clearing, it's essential to clear the people! Once your pendulum tells you the space is in a clear and balanced state, then do personal clearings for everyone who lives there. If you run out of time or feel too tired, you can wait till later to do so, but don't put it off for more than one day. (If you cleared a friend's house and can't go back to meet with them in person, you can clear them from a distance.) Once the space and the beings in it are in coherence, life is full of new possibilities!

The Final Step: Placing the Discerning Energy Field (DEF)

You've cleared your home and the people in it, but what about anything *outside* the house that might be infiltrating to stress your system? What if there's a cell phone tower nearby that's affecting you in your space? What if you live down the street from a medical clinic, and the broadcast of energy from the staff and patients is strong enough that it's impacting you in your home? Or what if you just have a cranky neighbor who's sending negative thoughts into your space? There can be any number of factors outside your property that can influence you inside your house, and for this reason, the last step in any space clearing is to place what's called a Discerning Energy Field (DEF) around the house.

The DEF is not a protective bubble around you that keeps everything out. We don't want to shrink-wrap your house! Instead, you can imagine a beautiful golden filter glowing around your home, which screens out what would be detrimental for you but allows in what will be beneficial for your growth. It doesn't block out any difficult experiences that would advance your personal evolution—as we all know, many of our life challenges turn out to be invaluable for our development.

To set the DEF, you can simply imagine it forming, beginning as a tiny glow in the center of the house and expanding outward to encompass the entire property, but it can be a lovely experience to do a meditation instead. If you're doing the space clearing for a friend, it can be a beautiful ending to the session to lead them in a visualization to participate in forming the field. The following is one version you can use.

Guided Meditation to Set the Discerning Energy Field

Sit quietly and comfortably, and take a few deep breaths. Now imagine a spiral of beautiful golden loving light start to form in front of you. Picture this glowing light begin to slowly move toward you, and feel the gentle warmth and loving energy getting stronger. The closer the golden light gets to you, the more love you feel emanating from it.

Imagine now that you're stepping into the center of this energy field, letting it completely envelop you, wrapping you in this warm swirling light. Feel it embrace you and begin to fill your heart with love until your heart feels so full that it could overflow.

Take another deep breath, and now let this spiraling light overflow from your heart; feel it stream through your chest and down into your arms and hands and fingers. At the same time, it moves up your neck to warm your face and head. Then let it move down through your chest and into your lower body, your hips, down your legs, all the way to the tips of your toes. Your entire body is filled with warm, golden, loving light.

And now let this energy start to radiate out to fill the space around your body like a shining aura. Take a nice, deep breath. Then feel it begin to expand out to slowly fill the room, reaching every corner, every nook and cranny. Let it touch the walls, the floor, and the ceiling. When the room is full, the light begins to spread through the entire house, filling it completely with the bright glow of love. Take a few moments to imagine it now, swirling throughout the whole house.

When the house is full, imagine this golden radiance bursting out through the doors, the windows, and the roof to form a great field of light surrounding your home. Let it gradually grow to encompass the entire neighborhood if that feels right, and even larger if you want.

Now slowly bring this beautiful, pure luminosity back to surround just your property and your house, its outer edge stopping at the boundary of your land. Know that this will remain as a Discerning Energy Field to support and sustain the results of the clearing. It will act as a filter to screen out what is not needed for your personal growth, but allow in anything that you need in your life's journey.

Now take another deep breath, and feel your awareness returning back inside the house and then back to your own body. Feel the weight of your bottom in the seat of the chair, your feet on the ground. One more deep breath, and let yourself feel the peace and beauty of your home around you.

This is often a special experience for everyone that contributes to a real sense of the sacred in the space. After a few moments of quiet, you might explain to them that they can use this meditation again at any time to help refresh the energy in the space. Each time they do it, it not only resets and strengthens the Discerning Energy Field but also makes them feel more connected to the spirit of their home.

This can be important because it's the responsibility of the people living in the house to maintain the integrity of the space clearing. In other words, the clearing you just performed opened up all kinds of new possibilities and opportunities for their lives and has even created a new template in which they could frame their experiences. They can seize the chance to remain at that level and even keep improving from there, or they could regress and start filling the space with their own personal dramas again.

Checking the Status of the DEF

The effects of most space clearings last at least a year. I've checked back on many I did years ago and the energy is still holding. But if the people living there choose to continue as they have in the past, the clearing may last only a few months or so. Or if something really difficult or traumatic happens there later on, it can of course create new imbalance.

After some time has passed since the clearing, you can use your dowsing rod to check the status of the Discerning Energy Field. This is an interesting exercise that provides a visual to see how well the new energy is holding.

Stand inside the front door and start to walk toward the street, telling yourself you're looking for the outer boundary of the DEF. If the rod turns before you reach the property line, it means the DEF has started to shrink; the clearing is not holding. Sometimes you'll find the boundary's on the front porch, or even just inside the front door—or you won't find it at all.

If the DEF shrinks, this can be an indication that emotions have been building up inside again, or it may even be there's some new GS or technology affecting the space. Sometimes all you have to do is repeat the DEF meditation to bring balance back. Other times it may require a new space clearing, but it probably won't take very long, since you'd cleared it so recently!

Michael's Space Clearing

One of the most profoundly moving space clearings I did was for Michael, a 27-year-old man who'd been diagnosed with schizophrenia when he was 18. He'd been a very talented, creative teen with a high IQ and a brilliant future. Then the illness devastated his life. When I met him, he was severely overweight, heavily medicated, and often on suicide watch.

His mother was the one who asked me to do the clearing in the hope it could help the situation. For the past year, his mother had tried to let Michael live on his own, renting a small house for him, though she had to come each day to make sure he was okay. But the experiment was failing. His sense of reality was severely distorted, and he wasn't making good choices. He'd let street people live with him who'd done drugs in the house and were abusive to him.

When I arrived and evaluated Michael, I really doubted I could have much impact on what was obviously a very bad situation. He was barely lucid and often didn't understand what I was saying even though I spoke slowly and simply. Using my Chinese face-reading skills, I could tell he was extremely sensitive to subtle energy, and so as I started clearing, I kept it very gentle so the shifts wouldn't be too difficult for him to feel. But even then, he soon felt overwhelmed and could only sit in a chair and watch me.

The living room was intensely full of imbalances, and I got vivid images of disturbed people sleeping on the floor and hanging out. My dowsing rod spun like crazy by the couch, and Michael's mother said, "That's where those people shot up drugs."

As I walked along one of the walls, I got a sensation that's become familiar to me as an indicator that there's a ghost in the space. I often use my hand as a sensing instrument in addition to my dowsing rod because I can feel energy, and it helps me get more the information about a disturbance. When I encounter a ghost, I sometimes feel what's like a spherical shape, and that's what I felt pressed up against the wall. It was almost as if he was trying to be flat enough that I didn't notice him!

As Michael observed me, he said, "Ask him if his name is Henry." He could see the ghost; he knew he was there, even though I hadn't commented out loud that I'd found one. This was a very sensitive young man. Well, the ghost's name wasn't Henry, but he was definitely stuck there in the house and actually very eager to find freedom, as most ghosts are. It took only a few moments for him to transform and disappear from the space.

I continued to clear the rest of the house, discovering both massive geopathic stress and technology adversely affecting Michael's sensitive system. He began to feel so overcome by all the energy changes that he went to lie down in bed. At the end, I asked him if he felt well enough for me to do a personal clearing for him, and he shyly said, "Oh yes, please, as long as you don't mind if I just lie here." This was such a lovely guy, and my heart went out to him.

I sat at Michael's bedside, and as I began to clear, it felt like the boundaries of my heart and mind and entire energy system shot wide open. It was as if light from heaven flowed through me and into him. I was no longer there; it was just God's love streaming into Michael. It was one of the most remarkable experiences I've had with clearing. But even after that amazing time, I left wondering if I'd been any help at all. This was such a dire situation that I doubted simple energy work could make a dent.

Several weeks later, I got a voice mail. The man's voice seemed only vaguely familiar, but then he said his name: Michael. Instead of sounding barely lucid, he was articulate and energized: "Jean, I just wanted to thank you for all your help. Since you did the clearing, I'm now off all my meds, and I've lost 60 pounds. My mother no longer has to check on me every day, and she's taking her first vacation in 10 years. And I won a poetry competition that gave me a scholarship to a program I'm on my way to right now. I can't thank you enough!"

Who knows how much, if anything, the space clearing contributed to this transformation for Michael. We can never know what will happen as a result of a clearing, nor can we claim credit. But in that moment, all that mattered to my heart was this beautiful guy's life had gotten so much better.

Frequently Asked Questions (FAQs)

Just like with learning personal clearing, there are common questions I get at this point in the training. So on the following pages, you'll find some helpful advice and answers to some questions you may have been wanting to ask!

"How often should I space-clear my house?"

In general, it's good to clear your space about once a year. However, if you've been through an exceptionally stressful time, you could ask your pendulum if the space is in a clear and balanced state. If you get a "no," then clear it! It will probably be a very quick session the second time around because you released so much previously.

Don't make the mistake that some beginners do, anxiously wondering if the space clearing might not have been good enough and so doing a second one soon after. This can actually cause havoc in the space, such as appliances breaking down or people having sleep problems. The energy needs time to settle and integrate. One of the most important lessons we learn through clearing is to trust the process and allow things to unfold.

"I love the energy in my grandmother's chair. I don't want to get that cleared!"

Clearing releases only energy that's stressed, that's adversely affecting you in your space. Your grandmother's chair is broadcasting beneficial energy, so don't worry; you won't lose the good juju!

"Should I go outside to clear in the garden?"

Our focus is on clearing the places where the people spend most of their time, so you aren't required to clear in the garden. The land won't hold much emotional residue because people aren't dumping their feelings there each day. And nature has its own clearing system with the wind, sun, rain, and plants all keeping energy moving!

Most of the time, when you clear GS in the house, that can also clear it throughout the property. But if you're an avid gardener, or want practice clearing, it can be a truly lovely experience to clear in the garden too!

"Is it okay for children to be present during a space clearing?"

I usually recommend that very small children be out of the house during a space clearing, but not because it's dangerous for them. Kids are very sensitive to energy and can go into reaction as things start to shift. Their acting up could distract you and interrupt the clearing.

If you can't do the clearing while the kids are at school or daycare, then have someone stay with them to keep them occupied the entire time you're clearing. Don't expect them to sit and watch a movie or play games on their own as they usually might!

"Can I do a space clearing if I'm ill?"

This isn't advisable. Clearing a space is more demanding than clearing a person. People hold back; they release just a little bit at a time as they're ready to. But an environment doesn't have any such resistance! So it can be too demanding for your system if you're physically compromised. It also takes longer to clear a place than a person, so if you're ill, you need to save your time and energy for getting well. Wait until you're healthy again, or bring someone else in to do the clearing.

"Can I just do a 'general' clearing of a house like I can do for a person?"

No, clearing a space is very different from clearing a person. If you tried to tune in to an entire house, you'd be opening up to far too much at one time, at least for your current level of knowledge. In my advanced trainings, you learn how to do remote space clearings, so you know how to manage how much energy you work with at any one time in a space.

However, for situations such as a hotel stay, you *can* just clear your hotel room; you don't have to clear the entire hotel! The Discerning Energy Field that you set at the end will filter out any detrimental influences outside the walls of your room. You'll probably be amazed at how well you sleep, especially after clearing the bed!

Another special situation during travel is when you're on an airplane. You can do a general clearing of the seat as you sit in it. Just tune in and hold the thought that you're clearing anything that would adversely affect you while you're there. You can surreptitiously hold your pendulum between your knees so your seatmate doesn't notice. You can also use a key ring as a temporary pendulum, and they'll just think you're fiddling with your keys. You may also find that clearing can often smooth out any turbulence if the plane starts to experience it!

SPACE-CLEARING FROM START TO FINISH

Here's an abbreviated step-by-step guide you can refer to when you do a space clearing. Please don't use this shorthand version until you've read and understood the full information covered in Part II.

1. Preliminaries

- Check to see if you're switched. (Remember to continue to check frequently throughout the space clearing.)

- Take a deep breath, relax, and become aware of your feelings.

- Ask if it's appropriate to proceed.

- Ask: "Is the qi in this space in a clear and balanced state?"

- If "no," ask: "Is it more yin than yang?" Find out the general ratio of yin to yang.

- Check to see if the qi is coming in the front door.

- Ask: "Is the Primary Disturbance on this property?" If "yes," locate and clear. If "no," find out in which direction the Primary Disturbance lies; determine whether it's due to emotion, geopathic stress, or technology; and then clear it from where you are.

- Return to the front door and dowse to see if there is any change as to how the qi may be entering.

2. Qi Flow

- Define your first search area, such as the foyer or the living room, and tell yourself you are now going to *follow the flow of qi* in that area.

- Walk with your dowsing rod until it turns you in a spiral or zigzags to indicate that you've found some stressed emotion held in the space.

- Clear the disturbance.

- Face your dowsing rod forward and follow the qi flow again, clearing each area of stress as you find it.

- When your dowsing rod has taken you through the entire room, then you're ready to check for geopathic stress.

3. Geopathic Stress (GS)

- Ask: "Is there any geopathic stress in this room affecting the people who live here?"

- If "yes," find out which of the three kinds of GS are present in the room: disturbed magnetic fields, faulting pressure, and/or stressed underground water.

- Walk the width and length of the room, mapping out where the lines of GS exist.

- For each one you locate, ask if it can be cleared. If "yes," clear it, and then go on to do the same for the rest. Do not attempt to clear more than one line of GS at a time.

- When you're finished clearing GS in a room, the last thing to do is check the adverse effects of technology.

4. Technology

- Ask: "Is there any technology in this room that's adversely affecting the people who live here?"

- If "yes," point to each device or appliance and ask if clearing is needed.

- Each time you get a "yes," clear it. You can imagine the disturbing field shrinking back into the device, if you like.

5. Completion

- Now return to following the qi flow, letting your dowsing rod take you out of the room you've just finished clearing and into another room in the house. Let the rod determine where you go next, because it's following the energy.

- Continue in the same way, room by room, through the rest of the house. In each room, clear emotional disturbances, GS, and adverse effects of technology, one by one as you find them, until you've been to each part of the space.

- Ask: "Is the qi in this space in a clear and balanced state?"

- If "no," find the areas that still hold stress and clear them. If "yes," continue on to do the personal clearings.

6. Personal Clearing

- Do personal clearings for each of the people who live in the space. If you're too tired, or if the people there are too tired at the end of the space clearing, you can do the personal clearings later in the day or the next day. You don't have to meet in person—you can clear them remotely—but don't wait longer than a day to do so.

7. Discerning Energy Field

- Do the visualization to form the Discerning Energy Field.

So now that we've made the journey through learning the step-by-step process of how to clear people and places, let's look at what this all means for a deeper understanding of what happens when you can just "be" with some energy rather than trying to "do" something about it.

part III

ACTIVATING the POWER of YOUR COMPASSIONATE HEART

❀ ❀ ❀

Each time we drop our masks and meet heart-to-heart,
reassuring one another simply by the quality of
our presence, we experience a profound bond which
we intuitively understand is nourishing everyone.
Each time we quiet our mind, our listening becomes sharp
and clear, deep and perceptive; we realize that we know more
than we thought we knew, and can reach out and hear,
as if from inside, the heart of someone's pain.
Each time we are able to remain open to suffering,
despite our fear and defensiveness, we sense a love in us
which becomes increasingly unconditional.

— Ram Dass

chapter 12

How and Why Does Clearing Work?

You've been learning powerful skills for how to clear energy. But as you've been doing this, something even more amazing is happening. *You* are being personally transformed in ways that are altering the course of the rest of your life. You're not only experiencing a training in changing energy; in the process, you are gently but deeply changing your body, mind, spirit—and your future.

It's like you're getting rid of the old programming and installing a powerfully updated version! This is a training for your entire system, one that changes your relationship with your life, your relationship with all your experiences, and all your patterns of thought and emotion. It is transforming how you walk through the world from here.

To understand how and why this happens, we need to look more deeply at what's really going on when you do a clearing. Let's look at what we know:

You are both a receiver and transmitter of energy. You're an open system in constant communication with your environment, affected by and affecting everything around you in ways that are often below your conscious awareness.

How are you affected by what you receive? You entrain to the energy in your surroundings, whether that's the background music playing in the restaurant or the mood of the person sitting in the office next to yours. In other words, you change in response to the vibrations around you.

And not only do you make those adjustments, but in many cases, your system is stressed just by experiencing those energies. When you're near someone who's tense, it's not only that you entrain to that tensed vibe. It's also an unpleasant feeling to deal with, and that puts extra demands on your daily workload, tiring you out a little bit more each time it happens.

How are you affecting the world around you? You broadcast your thoughts, feelings, and personal history like a radio station. You're running the same program day after day because of that continual story looping in your head. It's a message that others receive and react to, which can keep you locked into having the same experiences in your relationships. Why do you seem to keep dating the same kind of person over and over, or have repetitive problems with people at work? The experiences you have with others are a mirror showing you what your personal radio station is broadcasting and how people respond to that information.

So you are both a receiver and transmitter. But aside from what's happening in your external world, there's a third truth here: your inner world is also a powerful influence on you. That Pig-Pen-like cloud around you consists not only of the energetic "grime" you've taken on from the people and places in your life but also all the baggage you're carrying from your past: unresolved issues, self-defeating beliefs, old pain, all the "unloved" parts of you that you've not been able to embrace and integrate.

Why haven't you been able to come to a place of peace with these various parts of your history? Because you hold a charge around these feelings; there's tension built up in each one. Whenever you turn toward one, it hurts to touch that place. Then one of two things usually happens: you either quickly turn away to stop the feeling, or you get lost in it.

If you try to resist a feeling because it's too uncomfortable, you suppress it and stuff it down with the belief that if you don't allow yourself to feel it, you'll stay safe from that stress. But every time you make that choice, it just increases the tension you hold around it and makes it even more stuck in your field.

On the other hand, if you get lost in a feeling, you let it overwhelm you. You get swept out to sea, and then it can take minutes, hours, or days to swim back to shore. Every time this happens, it strengthens the synapses in your brain associated with that response, increasing the likelihood you'll get deeply lost in that emotion again the next time.

Whether they're suppressed or empowered, these unloved pieces accumulate and build up to create a thick filter through which you view everything about yourself and others. It limits you, keeps you stuck in patterns of belief and behavior, and obscures your vision about the possibilities for your future. Your beautiful inner light can be hard to discern through the layers of that heavy cloud!

Well, Now How About Some <u>Good</u> News?!

So we know you're affected by external energy. In your daily life, this is mostly a negative influence because you're surrounded by people who are broadcasting tension and stress. But the important truth here is you're affected by external energy! That means that if the external energy is welcoming, accepting, and kind, you will be affected in a positive way.

We know you affect others with your own energy. So all the work you've done on yourself to become a wise and loving person certainly does matter! But at the same time, you also communicate all the unhealthy beliefs you carry about yourself, and these transmit with a greater intensity. As you go through your normal day, anxious about money, stressed out about your weight, or feeling not good enough in so many ways, this all heavily colors the positive message you're trying to convey to others. But if you could set all that aside even for a moment and be with another person from more of a peaceful space, your effect on them would be life enhancing, even healing.

Finally, we know that inner story you're telling yourself is what's keeping you continually creating your future based on your past. You've been repeating it to yourself for so many years now, it's firmly engraved in your mind as reality. This is how you define yourself, what you believe your life to be; it's the room you live in. But what if you had a way to step outside of the confines of that room, even momentarily? How might that change your view of what's possible for you to become? What if you could even start breaking down its walls so you could eventually achieve a far more spacious place to stand in your life?

You've probably been trying to do that in various ways for years, but perhaps without as much progress as you'd like. You're a smart person—if your brain could have figured a way out, you'd have done it long ago. But the problem is that you're caught in this limiting world view that causes you to form solutions that are basically just a new version of the same thing. As Einstein said, "We can't solve problems by using the same kind of thinking we used when we created them." You need a way to step outside of the box you're in. In other words, you need to stop running that program that keeps you reacting to things in the same way time after time, and therefore getting the same results.

I mentioned earlier that there are two common responses you have when a thought or feeling rises in your system: to suppress it or to get swept away in it. But there's a third possible response: to allow it but not give it power. When you do that, it surfaces—and then moves on. This is a choice we rarely make, partly because we've not been taught how, but primarily because it's not so easy to be objective about our own experience. It's *our* feeling; it comes packaged with that energetic charge from our past.

But what if someone *else* was to tune in to allow that thought or emotion that holds tension for you? To them, it's just a piece of information, just some energy. It has no charge for them because it's not theirs. They didn't have the stressful experience it's associated with. It's not connected to any issue from their past; it has a totally different energetic frequency than any of their own personal pain. So they don't feel any impulse to resist it, and they certainly don't get swept away in it. Instead, they can easily make that third choice—to just be aware of it, to allow it, but without going into reaction. As author Geneen Roth so rightly said, "All any feeling wants is to be welcomed with tenderness."

This is what happens during a clearing. You connect with the energy of some stress in the other person's system, but because you have no history with that feeling, it's not challenging for you. So you can relate to it in an entirely different way than they have been. And in that process, the act of your welcoming and witnessing it releases it, lets it finally relax and disappear. Like massaging a tense muscle, or unkinking a garden hose, the discomfort, the blockage, is gone.

When you sit down to do a personal clearing for someone, you are consciously connecting with their energy. It's not like a situation in your regular life where you're being unknowingly affected by them—here, you're tuning in with a particular kind of awareness. There's a defined agreement, and because they've said "yes" to a clearing, their energy just naturally opens to you without their even trying. Due to the training you've received, you're purposefully opening to their energy in a calm, accepting frame of mind.

Then, as you pick up the pendulum, you drop into an additional state of being, potentially with all your brainwaves active at the same time and your consciousness automatically scanning for information. When your pendulum indicates you've located an area of stress held in that person's energy, it means you've encountered something "unloved" in their system. It's some tension held around an experience they had in the past, or a piece of their drama they so firmly believe is real, or a feeling they're resisting because it's too painful.

As you allow that feeling, as you greet it without resisting it or fueling it, it's no longer locked in place; it just moves on. It doesn't matter if you think you're not feeling anything when you do a clearing. You actually are; it's just that it's happening beneath your conscious awareness. The effect is still the same.

Entraining

Another way to look at what may be going on during a clearing is to understand that your two energies naturally entrain. We can look further at definitions of entrainment here to help us understand.

In physics, it's described as when one system slows down and the other accelerates until their frequencies are identical. This is because there's an energy transfer between them that they respond to by establishing a more and more stable relationship, and so they end up in a matching rhythm.

In geography, entrainment is said to be what happens when water surrounds soil and carries it away in its flow. In meteorology, entrainment occurs when one current of air envelops another and they become one. So, for example, we might visualize how this applies to what happens in a clearing when you tell your mind, "I'm clearing Disturbing Effects of Others." As your pendulum is swinging, your mind is scanning for those areas of stress held in that person's field. Then, when you find one, your awareness embraces that energy and carries it away like water does to the soil or like one breeze surrounding another to flow together.

Ancient Chinese medicine has a concept similar to entrainment but they call it "resonance." They believe the greatest physicians are ones who are able to harmonize their qi with the qi of the patient, like two temple bells sounding in unison; and in that moment, true healing happens.

One last important truth about the effects of entrainment: As you clear someone, you're actually creating a new energetic template for them, and giving their system a chance to reprogram itself. Each time you hold one stressed, unloved part of their energy in compassionate awareness, neither resisting it nor giving it power, you're subtly demonstrating to their unconscious self how they might choose to respond to their experiences from a place of acceptance and not reaction.

You don't have to say any of this out loud or try to explain it to them. Remember that through the process of entrainment, your frequencies come into coherence. This isn't a mental exercise, and that's why it has such power—because it's a direct energetic exchange happening beneath the surface of awareness.

Activating Your Compassion

As you sit and clear with a kind, receptive attitude, you're holding a compassionate place for that person's feelings to "be," just like a mother holding her child in her arms. Interestingly, in Semitic languages, the word for "compassion" is related to the word for "womb," which brings to mind the sense of a mother's love for her child. The archetype of Mother represents the one we turn to for comfort and understanding; she loves us and accepts us unconditionally, without judgment, no matter what we do. In Christianity, this loving Mother energy is represented by Mary, the mother of Jesus. In Chinese culture, the goddess of compassion is Quan Yin, whose original Sanskrit name translates as "She who hears the cries of the world," also conjuring an image of Mother. When things fall apart, you can always go home to Mother. It's the safest place in the world to be.

In a clearing, we activate the power of our compassion as we're available to hold the space for another's stressed feeling. Because of the way the process of clearing is designed, we can do it easily and naturally. Just as a mother doesn't greet her crying child by crying herself, but instead with a calm heart and a warm lap, we do the same for the person we're clearing.

As you practice clearing others, you'll become more and more able to effectively clear yourself because this new compassionate approach will also begin to extend to yourself. But even during this learning stage, what you may be surprised to find is that just in the act of clearing someone else, you end up feeling better yourself because of the time you've spent in that special state of mind.

Additionally, you're also learning a new energetic template for yourself. As you learn to transmute the charge someone else is carrying around a feeling, you're reprogramming how you respond to your own feelings as well. Every day your spirit becomes lighter and lighter. (We'll talk more about this in the next chapter.)

When you first start to learn to do clearings, you'll naturally have some level of hesitation. Perhaps you're anxious that you might feel something unpleasant, or you doubt your ability, worried that you're not going to be effective enough. Because this work seems so simple, it can be hard to believe you're really doing anything! This is a normal stage that everyone moves through, and that's part of the learning curve. As you get more practice, you'll relax into the process and have more confidence because you'll see and experience the results on so many levels.

Up to this point, I've been talking about personal clearing, but all these concepts also apply to a space clearing too, of course. Whether you're connecting to stress held in a person or an environment, it's all the same process. This could really be thought of as learning how to hold a place of peace and balance within yourself no matter what you encounter, which then directly affects the people and places around you.

This can be seen in the story Carl Jung was told by Richard Wilhelm, the sinologist whose translation of the I Ching introduced so many Westerners to ancient Chinese wisdom. At one point during Wilhelm's 25 years in China, there was a terrible drought and the situation became quite dire. Finally, the Chinese sought out a rainmaker, similar to a shaman, and brought him to their village to make his magic. He locked himself up in a house for three days, and then suddenly, on the fourth day, clouds appeared and there was a great snowstorm!

As the whole town rejoiced, Wilhelm went to speak to the rainmaker, to ask him how he did it. But the old man said he wasn't responsible for making the snow. Wilhelm replied, "But what have you done these three days?" The shaman's reply was that in this province, things were out of balance, which put him out of balance as well. It took him three days to get back into harmony, and then the environment naturally did too; so the precipitation came.

Clearing is really just about bringing balance back, either to a person or a space. In fact, the principles on which clearing is based may actually be very familiar to you. In the next chapter, we'll look more deeply at those to help you make even more sense of the practice.

chapter 13

Clearing

a new approach
to mindfulness

W hat I've been describing may sound familiar to you
if you've had any experience with the mindfulness
movement over the past few decades, thanks to brilliant
teachers like Jon Kabat-Zinn, Jack Kornfield, Sharon Salz-
berg, and many others who have made a long study of Buddhist meditation practices. Although clearing is not based
on Buddhism (or any religion), there are many parallels
with Buddhism's teachings *and* with its beneficial results.

Mindfulness techniques teach people how to observe
their thoughts and feelings and just "be" with them, rather
than suppress them or drown in them. Sound familiar? In
Buddhism, this is achieved through practicing meditation,
where you train yourself to sit quietly and just notice what

passes through your mind without giving power to it, to view your thoughts like clouds floating across the sky.

One student's description of her experience learning meditation is what you often hear from people who've benefitted from this practice: "I came to see that my thoughts were simply that: thoughts. I didn't have to judge them, act on them, or do anything about them. They were no more than 'events' that arose in my mind and then dispersed again. They did not, as I'd previously imagined, have the power to undo me."

Once people learn this technique in meditation, the next step is to try to use this way of being as they go through their daily life as well, to notice a feeling as it comes up but not go into their usual automatic reaction to it. Buddhism calls for taking a "sacred pause" to claim a moment of conscious awareness about what's happening inside, so there's an opportunity to choose a response. For example, if someone notices they've made a mistake, they might instantly tense up and think to themselves some version of, *Oh crap, I can't believe I did that; I'm so stupid!* But after studying mindfulness techniques, they might instead notice a mistake and then observe that a self-critical thought is rising in their mind. They might then think, *This is some tension and anxiety about having made that mistake.*

These two different choices have very different effects on their system. The first reaction floods their body with biochemicals that make physiological changes based on that negative message and strengthen the synapses in their brain, making it more likely they'll continue to cringe with self-critical feelings again with the next mistake. But in the second choice, they're observing the feeling instead of identifying with it. They're not even saying, "I *am* anxious and tense," which would have the same effect of convincing the body, mind, and spirit to become that way. They are instead recognizing the way they're feeling with a "this is" statement, and that helps their system not take it on.

Fortunately, there are an ever-increasing amount of studies showing how beneficial mindfulness is for stress reduction as well as emotional and physical health. When you can just accept a feeling, just "be" with it, you create a moment of peace. This is a very different outcome than what usually happens, when it brings you a moment of stress instead. Add up all the thoughts and emotions you go through in the course of a day, and you can see how a lot of little stresses can compile to disrupt any chance of a healthy balance.

We're not educated in how to "be" in our culture. All our values revolve around how to "do"—to achieve, to look for what's wrong and fix it, to get results. As soon as we reach one goal, we're taught to start toward the next one. Forward movement is the key to success! It's wonderful to have a sense of drive, but if we're in constant "drive" mode, it throws our systems out of balance, first on a spirit level, then an emotional one, and eventually a physical one as well.

Chinese medicine teaches the value of yin and yang in every aspect of life. All that *doing* is very yang, and that's great. But we need to balance it with equal time and energy devoted to yin: stillness, peace, and allowing ourselves to feel. In other words, *being*.

Doing and being are not only about your choices in your external life. They happen internally as well. If your mind is always racing with everything you have to get done, that can frazzle your energy and contribute to burnout, even if you're not acting on all those thoughts. Every time you have an internal reaction to a thought, some version of the "Oh crap!" response, it creates activity in your system, physiologically as well as mentally and emotionally. And that means you "do" something about it, even if you don't physically take action.

But if you can learn not to go into that kind of reaction, all that frenzied activity doesn't happen; your wires aren't fraying as they would otherwise. So on many levels, we can understand the value of learning to just "be" with a thought, to just observe it but not give it power. When you can do this, it's like making friends with your mind, and that brings a new sense of peace that can feel like water in the desert.

So people try to use mindfulness techniques to reeducate their system in how to respond to their experiences, and the thoughts and emotions they have, as they go through their day. But there are real struggles with this practice. The fact is that they've spent *years* creating their personal drama! These patterns of reaction have become a part of them, automatic reflexes engraved in their systems, and it's not so easy to try to mentally undo decades upon decades of that programming.

Additionally, those thoughts often are connected to memories or beliefs that are painful. If you're recalling the time you got fired or an argument with a friend, or are falling back into your story about being all alone when everyone else is in a relationship, it causes you discomfort. It's not easy to neutrally observe thoughts like those, and in most cases, your reaction is so immediate, it's often not possible to catch yourself before you fall in that hole. You may be able to get to the point where you notice soon after it's happened and crawl out! And that's certainly helpful, but by that point, at least some negative energy has been coursing through your system.

This is why it can take years of seriously practicing meditation before people begin to notice truly significant life changes as a result. Like all of us, they're just too programmed with those instantaneous reactions that come from a place below their conscious control.

Accelerated Meditation

This is where clearing may transform the principles of mindfulness into a practice that brings easier and much more immediate results. Remember the meditation teacher who compared clearing to "accelerated meditation"? Clearing takes that same practice but instead of applying it to your own thoughts and feelings, you do it with someone else's! This streamlines the process because it bypasses the issue of your having to confront your own "stuff."

It's really hard to not take your own thoughts and feelings seriously. To your mind, there's a *reason* you feel this way! You had that bad experience years ago . . . You've always struggled with self-worth . . . *Anyone* growing up with a father like yours would feel like this! You can practice and practice observing what comes up in your mind, but it can be like Sisyphus rolling that boulder up the hill, the same mental exercises every day.

You can absolutely benefit from using mindfulness techniques if you keep at it over time, but what if we took a slightly different approach—one that might bring results more quickly and effectively?

Clearing applies the same exercise that mindfulness offers but with someone *else's* thoughts. It's incredibly difficult to be objective about your own thoughts but far easier to hold that place for someone else's because you carry no personal tension around them.

When you do a clearing for someone, you make a connection with patterns of thought and emotion that are adversely affecting them. These have built up quite a charge in their system, but they don't have the same effect on you. These aren't your issues. And because of that, you can greet each one without tension or resistance; you have no fear of it because you know it's not going to stress you as it would them. It's just some information you've observed, and so you're able to stay in balance, which is the goal of mindfulness training.

So every time you do a clearing, it's also subliminally teaching your own system how to respond to your own stress in a different way. You're practicing mindfulness, but with someone else's mind! This process bypasses all the problems you'd normally encounter in a regular mindfulness practice of trying to deal with your personal patterns that you're so attached to.

Doing clearings for others is a training for you to develop a new way of being within your own life. Every time you clear a stress held in someone's energy, you're welcoming that feeling without resisting it or losing yourself in it. And at the same time, you are learning to do that for your own feelings too.

I remember how astonished I was to see results after doing clearing this way for just two weeks. I regularly went for long walks, not only for exercise but also to de-stress. However, what I was actually doing was spending the entire time ruminating on all my problems and trying to come up with new ideas about what to do. That was helpful, but I always seemed to end up with more on my to-do list after a walk, which then gave me more to worry about! Sure, it was valuable to blow off steam physically, and it was good to devote time to focus on problem-solving, but it was keeping me spinning in a loop of stress and worry.

Then the results of doing clearings and the subsequent training of my own mind started to kick in. I went for a walk, and an hour later, I returned home and realized that I hadn't had a stressful thought the entire time. In fact, I had gone for a walk, and . . . I'd walked. I hadn't been up in my head at all. I noticed the beauty of nature all around me, enjoyed the birdsong, felt the sunshine on my skin and the pleasure of exercising my body. I had been totally present. Afterward, I felt a coherent energy flowing through my system in a way I'd never experienced before. And, somehow, my to-do list got smaller.

What had happened? As I'd been doing clearings for other people, I was reprogramming my system, developing a new relationship with my own mind. Every time I embraced someone else's stress without giving it power, I was also beginning to translate that ability for my own use, to not give my own stressful thoughts and feelings power either.

Release and Transform

Remember Malcolm Gladwell's "walk the line" story in Chapter 2, and the two transformations you'll need to do that in your life? One was to release the old stress that was stuck in your energy, and the second was to transform how you react to new stress from this point onward. Receiving clearings accomplishes the first, to release old energy. *Giving* clearings brings you to the second transformation, to no longer react to your experiences as you have in the past.

As you practice knowing "It's just a feeling; it's just information" when you clear someone else, you reprogram your system to automatically respond from that place to your own feelings too. Rather than try to force this through directly grappling with your own story, this way it gets slipped under the door, so to speak, so it's effortless.

When I talk about accepting and allowing a feeling, that doesn't mean passive resignation, or ignoring everything that passes through your mind. Instead, this practice creates a new way to respond to your thoughts and feelings. You begin to develop an easier sense of discrimination, one that helps you know which feelings call for action and which should not be acted upon or given power because they're just supporting the drama you're trying to free yourself from.

This ability to choose to respond to your thoughts in a different way comes from a more conscious moment of choice. Remember how we talked about the fact that there's an instant when a feeling first starts to rise inside you? And in that tiny moment, you unconsciously choose whether to suppress the feeling, get lost in it, or allow it? As you practice doing clearings, that time period starts to expand in your awareness so it's no longer just a fraction of a second. Now it becomes a more spacious span of conscious awareness, where you observe the feeling coming and make a balanced decision about how to respond to it.

We can do a visualization to help understand this. Imagine you've just made a mistake and are immediately anxious about it. *Eek, I turned in that report with those typos in it!* Envision that as you're sitting there, a helium balloon with the word "anxiety" written on it floats up beside you. You grab onto that balloon's string, and off it carries you, up, up, and away! You're lost in anxiety—your body flooded with physiological changes, your emotional state ungrounded—and it can take minutes or hours to come back to earth again.

After practicing clearing for a while, you may find that the next time a mistake happens, you notice the balloon with "anxiety" on it rising up beside you but you *don't* grab onto its string. Off it floats without you. You're so proud of yourself for managing that feeling differently, but then a second anxiety balloon floats up, and you just instinctively grab that one and off you go again. Darn! But as you continue to do clearings, you further develop the ability to not go into reaction. You make a mistake, the balloon rises, and you don't grab on. Another balloon comes up, and still you don't reach for the string. Soon the space of time between the balloons becomes longer and longer, and still you're sitting there, centered and in balance while the feelings come and the feelings go.

You never had the opportunity to have a conscious moment of choice before because your reactions were so immediate and below the level of your awareness. But now, because of the training you've received, things are different. You are naturally developing that "sacred pause" that allows you to make the healthy response, not only to what passes through your mind but also to what you experience in your external world. You make a mistake and you fix it. No angst necessary.

Neuroscientist Jill Bolte Taylor, who wrote the wonderful book *My Stroke of Insight*, discovered that when you have an emotion, it takes only 90 seconds for it to be processed through your body and flushed out of your bloodstream. The only reason you would continue to feel anxious after 90 seconds is if you are making the unconscious choice to run that program again. She described the solution: "By paying attention to the choices my automatic circuitry is making, I own my own power and make more choices consciously." This is what clearing trains your system to do, but without the struggle it normally takes to try to deal directly with your internal programming.

Regain Your Adaptability

As you become less and less stuck in old patterns, your energy regains its vibrancy and is free to flow with new resilience and flexibility. Chinese medicine defines health as "aliveness and newness moment to moment." Ancient texts described life as being a perpetual changing—a constant process of adaptation. The more we're able to go with the flow of events, the more in balance and healthy we are, physically, emotionally, and spiritually.

Chinese physicians believed that the only times the qi of your body, mind, and spirit is perfect are the moment after your birth and the moment before your death; every moment in between is a matter of adapting to changing circumstances. You can visualize it as if you're balancing on a surfboard, riding the waves. Your original self arrived here with that ability, but most of what's happened since you arrived has diminished it, and that's affected how well you can stay in balance. You have baggage, and if you're on a surfboard carrying baggage, it's pretty difficult to not tumble off into the water!

To regain the inner adaptability that allows you to adjust to whatever comes your way, two things are required: let go of your baggage, and don't take any more on! As you clear what's been stuck in your energy, you're releasing layers of that heavy burden you've been carrying for so many years. Simultaneously, you're developing a new relationship with your own thoughts, feelings, and reactions in life, and so you're less likely to take on new baggage. You gain a new lightness of spirit, and the ability to dance with life changes rather than struggle with them.

It's fascinating that the ancient Chinese pictograph for the word "sage" or "master" is an image of a dancing child! In her brilliant book, *Five Spirits*, alchemical acupuncturist

Lorie Dechar says that Taoists alchemists regarded the "ultimate goal of a human being's psychospiritual journey" to be "the return to original nature," or "the birth of the sage." From this, she says, comes the ancient origin of the character.

The Chinese character for the word *tzu*, master or sage, is a picture of a dancing child. The character reinforces the idea that the master is one who has returned to origin, someone who is capable of combining the wisdom of experience with the unbroken spontaneous innocence of a child.

The ancient and modern Chinese characters for Sage.

What a lovely image to hold in your mind, the sage in a state of aliveness and newness from moment to moment like a dancing child. *This* is where clearing can take you.

Next, let's look at the stages you'll move through as you learn this work, as well as some real-life stories that can inspire you as you move into this new way of being.

chapter 14

Stages of Learning

There are predictable stages you'll go through with this work. At first, you'll likely struggle to feel confident that you're doing anything at all. In fact, the biggest challenge people tend to have with clearing in the beginning is that it's so simple, it's hard to believe anything's happening. So if that's how you're feeling at this point, congratulations: you're right on schedule!

As you continue to practice and gain experience, you'll get past that phase because you'll start to see results. You'll feel noticeably different after getting or giving a clearing. Things will happen after a session that range from tiny changes to mind-boggling developments. You'll start to recognize that your own daily life is transforming, just as a consequence of the training you're receiving, effortlessly, as you do clearings. You'll be far less stressed by what used to stress you because the tension around that thought, feeling, or memory has been released, and you're developing a different way of relating to your new experiences.

Gradually, life becomes full of ease, grace, and a natural sense of joy.

It may sound strange, but I suggest that you start out clearing people you don't know well. This is because you have so much personal knowledge about your close friends and family, it's very easy to have a judgment about what you think is right for them! This can prevent you from being in an open, receptive state of mind during the clearing, or even make you have an attachment to its outcome. You *know* your husband should just be better organized so he won't be late for everything, and that belief can infiltrate the clearing you do for him. It may very well be true, but there may be other things that need to clear and other outcomes that need to emerge before he suddenly starts showing up on time!

So it can be helpful to start out by clearing acquaintances. But having said that, I do have to add that it can be a beautiful experience to clear those dearest to you since you already love them so completely. You naturally have strong feelings of compassion for your own child, for instance, so you can already hold such a more expansive space for them than you could for a stranger. So don't disregard clearing the people you love; it's wonderful to do so. Just practice on others as well, so you can develop your ability to stay objective.

No Attachment to the Outcome

One mistake many people make in their journey with this work is to focus on the problem presented or the result that seems obvious to aim for. In other words, if you're clearing a friend who is suffering from a broken heart or has a health problem, it's so tempting to think the right thing to do is "clear so she can find forgiveness" or "clear his kidney problem."

Any of these intentions, though sincere and full of love, come colored with a very limited understanding of how energy actually works. So, again, a reminder that you can't possibly know what needs to happen for balance to return. It may be that something entirely different has to come up for clearing first—some ancient pain or trauma that you couldn't possibly know about, or some other issue that needs to be resolved—before change can happen with the emotional or physical problem that your friend is dealing with currently.

And watch out for your own personal judgment that the situation is "bad" and therefore has to be eradicated. When you look back at your own history, can you see how often what seemed "bad" at the time actually was a very necessary stage in a process that brought you to a wonderful new level in your life, and without it, you'd have never gotten there?

Even more important is the fact that if you're clearing with the belief that a certain outcome is desirable, or if you're trying to "send love and healing," you are "doing," forcing your own energy on the situation. No matter how well intentioned, your personality is intruding where it does not belong.

Here's what to do: just clear. If you need to have an "intention," then just let it be for balance to return. If you're worried about what thought to hold in your mind, remember, that's already part of the protocol. You are clearing a certain field, so hold in mind, *I'm clearing Metal* or *I'm clearing this disturbed magnetic field*—wherever you are in the process of a personal clearing or space clearing.

We are so conditioned to think we have to figure out how to get what we want, and that's what's gotten us into this mess in the first place! Remember that boy when you were 16? That boy who you knew was your one true love and that your life would be over if you didn't marry him? And now you thank your lucky stars that you never married him because he's doing 20 years in prison! We have such a narrow view at any moment of what's right for us, and often what we so earnestly desire is just a reflection of our current imbalance, or of the degree of personal evolution we've achieved so far.

Sometimes people are too shy to ask for clearings, so they only give them. This is a great way to get tons of experience, but it's essential to *get* cleared as well. If you're showing up still carrying years of your own stress and tension, you will not be able to hold much of a space for the person you want to clear. The more you can show up "empty," the more effective you'll be with this work. Recognize how your own personal patterns of not wanting to impose, or difficulty with receiving, may be preventing you from finding balance, not only with this work but also in life overall.

The good news is that there's a worldwide community of people already trained and available to practice clearings with you! You can connect with them at: www .facebook.com/clearhomeclearheart.

The Four Stages of Learning

Please pace yourself, and don't go around space-clearing every house in the neighborhood or clearing everyone you know in the first few weeks, no matter how enthusiastic you feel! This is powerful work, and the simplicity of it can be deceptive. When you do a clearing, energy is flying around, and things are invisibly shifting and transforming on many levels.

You need to gradually develop your abilities with lots of practice and experience over time, or you can soon feel overwhelmed. If you were climbing Mount Everest, you wouldn't go to the top in one direct climb; you'd stop at base camps along the way, to get used to the new altitude! It's like this with clearing too. You need to get used to new levels of expertise before you can move on to the next.

Western psychology defines four stages of learning something as: (1) unconscious incompetence, (2) conscious incompetence, (3) conscious competence, and (4) unconscious competence. When you first picked up this book, you were in a stage of "unconscious incompetence." You didn't know how to do clearing and you may not have ever heard of subtle energy.

The next phase is "conscious incompetence," kind of a training-wheels stage, where you're at the start of the learning curve. You're aware you don't know how to do it and you're just beginning to figure it out. Then comes "conscious competence," where you've learned the how-to, but doing it takes a lot of your concentration to stay on track and remember what to do when.

Finally, the last phase, "unconscious competence," is when clearing becomes effortless and automatic. You can do it while carrying on a conversation. You walk into a room where some stress is stuck, and the stress just melts away because it's second nature for you to clear it without having to think about it. Just your presence brings balance back.

So after you've gotten enough experience with this work, you may discover that at times you're dropping into clearing mode without even picking up a pendulum. What I found in my own life after doing clearings for a while was that whenever I encountered stressed energy, my system just started clearing because of how it had been trained. So if I'm sitting next to someone who's stressed in an airport, or if I walk into a store where the energy's out of balance, I find myself starting to yawn, and I feel the clearing happening automatically. (Remember, yawning is a common symptom of clearing.) Of course, the people around me must just think I didn't get much sleep the night before!

This doesn't mean you're going to be out of control, with clearing coming over you at any moment! If I'm driving or it's not appropriate for me to be clearing for any reason, I simply tell my system that I'm not open for business right now, and that ends that. I do still use my pendulum each time I sit down to purposely do a clearing, as continual practice for my sensitive self to regulate how open I am to any particular energy at any one time.

Clearing Stories

The following are some examples of the kinds of stories I hear from people after they learn how to clear. They may inspire you to clear in your own life!

Kristy was awakened the morning after attending a clearing workshop by a strange sound in her kitchen. She jumped out of bed and ran toward the noise, only to see a man trying to crawl in the kitchen window! She screamed at him, and startled, he backed out and ran away.

But Kristy felt furious that he'd tried to violate her home. Her eyes landed on the dowsing rod she'd left on the kitchen table after coming home from the training, and she grabbed it. *If I can use this to find information in an environment,* she thought, *then maybe I can track down this burglar!*

She walked out of her house holding the rod, not even caring what the neighbors might think to see her walk down the street in her pajamas, pointing a metal rod in front of her! She held in mind the thought, *Take me to the guy who just tried to get into my house.* The rod led her on a winding route for a few blocks and then into the parking lot of an apartment complex where it turned, indicating she'd arrived at the location she was asking for.

She stood there, looking around, suddenly feeling quite foolish. There was no one in sight. *Oh well,* she thought. *It was worth a try.* Then in the next moment, the door to the apartment building opened, and out walked the man who'd just tried to break into her home! When he spotted her, he quickly dashed back inside.

Even though she knew the police wouldn't act if she told them her story, she felt triumphant that her dowsing skills were already so good after just a weekend workshop. In fact, the history of dowsing has several examples of criminals being captured because someone was able to track them with a dowsing rod!

There are so many ways we can use this work. William space-cleared his home and then thought, *Why not give it a try with my car?* So he just sat in the car, held the thought in mind that he was clearing any imbalances there and let his pendulum tell him when the clearing was complete. Because he had always kept careful records of his gas mileage, he was able to see in the weeks after the clearing that he got 25 percent better mileage than before!

Shannon's e-mail to me is typical of the ones I get from parents on a regular basis:

> *I'm so thrilled that I can clear my children, and I'm seeing how it benefits them in so many ways. My son used to have anxiety attacks and these have disappeared, and my daughter now comes to me when she's upset and says, "Mommy, will you clear me?" rather than throwing a tantrum. I feel empowered as a parent with this work.*

Grace wrote to me about her experience with a medical emergency with her child:

> *Our family went camping last weekend in the mountains and did a hard hike on the second day. Both of my children have Type 1 diabetes, so keeping them hydrated is crucial. But the hike, combined with the altitude we were at, definitely took a toll on everyone's hydration.*
>
> *That evening, unbeknownst to us, my daughter's insulin pump failed, which meant she didn't get any insulin for eight hours. So the next morning, she woke up in ketoacidosis—a dangerous situation which normally meant rushing to the hospital and an overnight stay. But we were eight hours away from home in the middle of nowhere!*
>
> *I decided to try clearing her. Then a miracle happened: within two hours, she dropped from a very high level of ketones to a manageable level and was even able to keep some fluids down. We've been in this*

scenario with our kids a few times and have never seen this happen. Usually it takes more than a day to get things under control and always with a hospital stay and an IV.

I'll never know for certain if it was due to my clearing, but in my heart, I believe it was. I'm just so grateful and amazed to know this work!

Donna bought a dozen roses to celebrate the event of her space clearing and couldn't believe her eyes when two weeks later, they were still as fresh as that first day. She continued to report to me that over the next *three months*, not only did the flowers survive and the water in the vase stay crystal clear the entire time, but also the stems were sprouting new buds and growing roots!

I've heard so many stories from people that they clear their animals and now their dog won't go to sleep at night until they've cleared him, or their "schizo cat" has become calm and affectionate. One woman cleared the geopathic stress in her garden and soon found birds flocking there, some of which weren't even common to her area. She set up a camera with a telephoto lens and ended up starting a new business selling images of the birds as greeting cards and framed prints. Her intention when she first came to my workshop was to clear the way for a new career. It certainly happened in a manner she could have never expected!

I've received anecdotal reports from oncology nurses who cleared their chemotherapy patients during treatment and found they had few to none of the usual side effects and much faster recovery times. And I constantly hear from people about clearing colds and flus within hours, and other seemingly miraculous resolutions of more serious health issues through repeated clearings, though of course we can never know if this was the reason.

People with allergies and food or environmental sensitivities often find relief through this work. One woman said, "I was so sensitive, I used to get severe, crippling migraine headaches with nausea and fatigue from eating food with even a trace of MSG in it. Even a taste of salad dressing or potato chips made me ill for days. Now I just tune in and clear my food before I eat it, and this no longer happens! It's been life-changing to be able to eat in restaurants again."

Countless people have found their weight dropped without any new diet or exercise after attending a clearing workshop. It makes you wonder how much of the weight many of us carry around is held there more for energetic reasons than anything else. Interestingly, I've always found that at clearing retreats, we eat like crazy yet don't seem to gain weight!

Savvy real-estate agents have space clearers on call for their difficult properties. I've heard so many accounts of bidding wars the day after a space clearing on a property that had been stuck on the market with no offers, or a sale that had fallen through suddenly getting back on track. More and more people are giving a space clearing as a gift for the new owners of their homes or having their own new place cleared as the first priority once they move in. (It's best to space-clear a new home after you've moved your belongings in so everything can get cleared all at once.)

Probably what's most dear to my heart are all the messages that pour in from highly sensitive people who say learning to clear has completely turned their lives around.

Diane wrote to me: "I used to come home from work and need the entire rest of the evening just to recuperate from having to cope with other people's energy all day. Now I'm no longer an energy sponge! For the first time in my life, I can say it's no longer hard to be me in the world."

Remember that each time you pick up your pendulum, your system is learning how to deliberately open up to energy. Each time you put down your pendulum, you're being trained in how it feels to put your boundaries back in place again. (For many highly sensitive people, this will be the first time they actually learn *how* to establish and control their energetic boundaries.) Soon you will naturally use this new ability in your everyday life, even when you're not using a pendulum as your on/off button.

But it's not just that this work helps highly sensitive people manage better. To me, just finding a way to survive in this intense world is not good enough! There's yet another level that you'll move to, one where it's actually a beautiful experience to be able to feel so much. Life becomes filled with sensual delights in every moment because you're finally safe enough to actually enjoy whatever you feel. Nothing will challenge your system; you can dance with the energy of every person or place that you encounter.

Sometimes people say to me, "It must be a nightmare for you to be so open and have to feel so much!" And yes, it used to be a constant overwhelm for me. But now, it's the opposite—just a gorgeous diversity of fascinating information always swirling around me, and I can be at ease with and love all of it. I wish the same for you.

It's always fascinating to hear from people about *their* clearing stories, and I've created a special e-mail address where you can write me privately to share your experience: mystory@jeanhaner.com. No experience is too trivial, so don't be shy about getting in touch with a confidential message. I look forward to hearing from you!

Uploading and Downloading Bliss

You've gotten so used to telling yourself a very limited story about who you are. That was not who you arrived to be, and it's not who you really are now. To reclaim your original nature, you need to let go—let go of the story, and of the patterns of reactions you've become stuck in. In order to be successful, this has to be done gradually, gently, and in an honoring way.

With each clearing you receive, tiny aspects of your unloved side are being accepted with ease. With each clearing you give, you are learning a new way of being in your own life. As the layers of that cloud around you slowly evaporate, your bright inner luminosity gets more and more apparent, and others around you respond to that light. As you move beyond the limiting room you've been confined in, as the walls fall away, you become a spacious being living a spacious life.

And in the process, your heart expands its range, its ability to love. The courageous heart is able to be open because it knows how to dance with anyone and anything it encounters. Each time you embrace the energy of a little feeling for someone else in a soft, receptive way, your heart is learning how to be safe with everything you feel in your own life. This is the way to becoming a fully compassionate presence wherever you go. With each clearing you give and receive, you're further activating the power of your heart, and that not only helps your personal evolution; it can change the world.

You have within you an extraordinary capacity for love and joy that is just waiting to be given a chance to emerge more fully. Remember my experience of uploading and downloading bliss because I had connected to the energy of the powerful healers and teachers who were also supporting my friend as she was dying? Since that moment, I've carried the vision of creating the same kind of network for all of us to tap into whenever we need it. When people join together with the simple intent to bring balance, they entrain with one another, harmonizing effortlessly and beautifully, and so they all benefit; they are all transformed.

Clear Home, Clear Heart Community

This network of people devoted to clearing is already available to you online, and it is growing as this book reaches the hands of many all over the world. I'd love to invite you to help us all be present for one another in this way. I hope you'll visit me at www.jeanhaner.com and www.facebook.com/clearhomeclearheart. There you can ask questions, find a clearing partner, or request clearings for yourself or anyone as well as continue to learn more about this work.

I encourage you to play with what you've learned in this book, and to be easy on yourself as you develop your skills and understanding. Don't have expectations that you'll do it all perfectly right from the beginning, and try not to be disappointed if you don't get instant results! Avoid pushing yourself to do too much, and remember that just because clearing seems so easy, it doesn't mean it's not powerful. You will think you're not doing anything, but I assure you—you are!

I also hope that you'll consider learning more in person. Sometimes, I've found that even when people read my books more than once, it's not until they come to a retreat or workshop that everything falls into place. Suddenly, they have the huge "aha!" where they finally feel confident that they know what they're doing. There's nothing like a real in-person experience. The energy of the group entraining together makes the learning far more powerful and life-changing. I've also seen over the years how many beautiful and lasting friendships have come out of the community of people who attend these classes! So please view my upcoming courses listed on the Events page at www.jeanhaner.com; I'd love to meet you and work together.

There's so much more to share with you—this is just the beginning, and I am so happy and honored to be by your side, two temple bells resonating together.

RESOURCES

Special gift just for readers of this book: www.jeanhaner.com/freegift

Free clearing videos and ways to learn more: www.jeanhaner.com
/clearingvideos

Resources for highly sensitive people: www.jeanhaner.com
/highlysensitivepeople

Resources for parents of highly sensitive children: www.jeanhaner
.com/highlysensitivechildren

Facebook community: *Clear Home, Clear Heart with Jean Haner*:
www.facebook.com/clearhomeclearheart

Certified clearing practitioners: www.jeanhaner.com/sessions

Dowsing supplies: www.jeanhaner.com/dowsingsupplies

Recommended Reading

Archetypal Acupuncture: Healing with the Five Elements,
by Gary Dolowich

Between Heaven and Earth: A Guide to Chinese Medicine,
by Harriet Beinfield and Efrem Korngold

*Chinese Medicine for Maximum Immunity: Understanding the Five Elemental
Types for Health and Well-Being*, by Jason Elias and Katherine Ketcham

The Diamond Cutter: The Buddha on Managing Your Business and Your Life,
by Geshe Michael Roach and Lama Christie McNally

The Divining Mind: A Guide to Dowsing and Self-Awareness,
by T. Edward Ross and Richard D. Wright

*Dogs That Know When Their Owners Are Coming Home:
And Other Unexplained Powers of Animals,* by Rupert Sheldrake

Entangled Minds: Extrasensory Experiences in a Quantum Reality,
by Dean Radin

Five Spirits: Alchemical Acupuncture for Psychological and Spiritual Healing,
by Lorie Eve Dechar

Miracles of Mind: Exploring Nonlocal Consciousness and Spiritual Healing,
by Russell Targ and Jane Katra

Practical Taoism, by Thomas Cleary

The Web That Has No Weaver: Understanding Chinese Medicine,
by Ted J. Kaptchuk

When the Body Says No: Exploring the Stress-Disease Connection,
by Gabor Maté, M.D.

*The Wisdom of Your Child's Face: Discover Your Child's True Nature with
Chinese Face Reading,* by Jean Haner

The Wisdom of Your Face: Change Your Life with Chinese Face Reading!,
by Jean Haner

The Wise Heart: A Guide to the Universal Teachings of Buddhist Psychology,
by Jack Kornfield

Wood Becomes Water: Chinese Medicine in Everyday Life,
by Gail Reichstein

Your Hidden Symmetry: How Your Birth Date Reveals the Plan for Your Life,
by Jean Haner

ACKNOWLEDGMENTS

A huge thank-you to my son, Jeffrey Wai-Ming Dong, who created the illustrations for this book. The artistic talent in my family definitely skipped a generation, bypassing me and going directly from my mother to him.

I'm also incredibly grateful for the multitude of brilliant insights from my editor, Nicolette Salamanca Young, who is a delight to work with and saved me from making a fool of myself in many places in this book. Deep gratitude as well has to go to Ruth Mikos for standing by me for so many years and making sure we stay on track, despite the sometimes complicated life I lead. And as always, my heart goes out to Louise Hay, who brought me into the Hay House family and with whom I've had so many adventures over the years.

I have many, many other people to give deep bows to, but most of all I want to thank all my teachers through the years, some of whom didn't show up in the form of a teacher. A special thank-you to William Bloom for long ago telling me to beware of men in uniforms, even those in monk's robes.

ABOUT the AUTHOR

Jean Haner is an intuitive empath, able to physically feel and work with the energy of people and places. Highly sensitive as a child, she easily absorbed the energy of others and also was overly affected by the vibrations held in environments. But through 30 years of training, research, and experience, she transformed her sensitivity from a challenge into a strength and developed the power to work with energy on a very refined level.

Because of her personal experience with both the challenges and benefits of being an empath, Jean is well known as a compassionate and effective teacher. She offers Clear Home, Clear Heart retreats and trainings and teaches Discover Your Inner Design workshops based on her three other Hay House books: *The Wisdom of Your Face, The Wisdom of Your Child's Face,* and *Your Hidden Symmetry.*

For information on courses, retreats, professional trainings, consultations and private sessions, please visit: www.jeanhaner.com.

Hay House Titles of Related Interest

YOU CAN HEAL YOUR LIFE, the movie,
starring Louise Hay & Friends
(available as a 1-DVD program and an expanded 2-DVD set)
Watch the trailer at: www.LouiseHayMovie.com

THE SHIFT, the movie,
starring Dr. Wayne W. Dyer
(available as a 1-DVD program and an expanded 2-DVD set)
Watch the trailer at: www.DyerMovie.com

FROM MY HANDS AND HEART:
Achieving Health and Balance with Craniosacral Therapy,
by Kate Mackinnon

THE POWER OF ATTENTION:
Awaken to Love and Its Unlimited Potential with Meditation,
by Sarah McLean

REMEMBERING THE LIGHT WITHIN:
A Course in Soul-Centered Living,
by Mary R. Hulnick, Ph.D., and H. Ronald Hulnick, Ph.D.

SOLE GUIDANCE:
Ancient Secrets of Chinese Reflexology to Heal the Body,
Mind, Heart, and Spirit,
by Holly Tse

THE THREE SISTERS OF THE TAO:
Essential Conversations with Chinese Medicine, I Ching, and Feng Shui,
by Terah Kathryn Collins

All of the above are available at your local bookstore,
or may be ordered by contacting Hay House (see next page).

We hope you enjoyed this Hay House book. If you'd like to receive our online catalog featuring additional information on Hay House books and products, or if you'd like to find out more about the Hay Foundation, please contact:

Hay House, Inc., P.O. Box 5100, Carlsbad, CA 92018-5100
(760) 431-7695 or (800) 654-5126
(760) 431-6948 (fax) or (800) 650-5115 (fax)
www.hayhouse.com® • www.hayfoundation.org

Published and distributed in Australia by: Hay House Australia Pty. Ltd., 18/36 Ralph St., Alexandria NSW 2015 • *Phone:* 612-9669-4299
Fax: 612-9669-4144 • www.hayhouse.com.au

Published and distributed in the United Kingdom by:
Hay House UK, Ltd., Astley House, 33 Notting Hill Gate, London W11 3JQ
Phone: 44-20-3675-2450 *Fax:* 44-20-3675-2451 • www.hayhouse.co.uk

Published and distributed in the Republic of South Africa by:
Hay House SA (Pty), Ltd., P.O. Box 990, Witkoppen 2068
info@hayhouse.co.za • www.hayhouse.co.za

Published in India by: Hay House Publishers India, Muskaan Complex, Plot No. 3, B-2, Vasant Kunj, New Delhi 110 070 • *Phone:* 91-11-4176-1620
Fax: 91-11-4176-1630 • www.hayhouse.co.in

Distributed in Canada by: Raincoast Books, 2440 Viking Way, Richmond, B.C. V6V 1N2 • *Phone:* 1-800-663-5714 • *Fax:* 1-800-565-3770
www.raincoast.com

Take Your Soul on a Vacation

Visit www.HealYourLife.com® to regroup, recharge, and reconnect with your own magnificence. Featuring blogs, mind-body-spirit news, and life-changing wisdom from Louise Hay and friends.

Visit www.HealYourLife.com today!